get happy!

by Jo Howarth

The **essential** daily guide to a mindful, happy life

Carliann,

Enjoy!

Jo x

First published in 2016
by The Happiness Club Ltd

Copyright © Joanna Howarth 2016

ISBN <978-1523288922>

Dedications

To my amazing husband and children:
You are at the heart of everything I do,
I love you more than the world.

To the members of The Happiness Club:
Thanks for coming on this journey with me.

To all my clients, past, present and future:
Thank you for trusting me.

To Vishvapani:
Thank you for sharing with me
the magic of Mindfulness.

And to my guide, my mentor, my teacher Eamonn:
Without you *none* of the things mentioned above
would be possible; my gratitude is eternal.

Contents

i

Foreword

There are some things you can't make happen.

You can't make yourself fall asleep if you're still wide awake well after bedtime – the harder you try, the less likely it is to happen. You can't make people like you. And you can't make yourself happy. That creates a puzzle because sleep, friendship and happiness are important parts of our lives.

It's hard to say what happiness is, exactly, but we all know what it feels like. Maybe other words get closer to the feeling for you – contentment, joy, elation, fulfillment. But whatever we call it, a deep wish to be well, happy and to flourish seems to be built in to our hearts and minds. So the puzzle is, how we can move towards happiness when we know we can't force it to happen?

Part of the answer is to stop doing the things that get in the way. Maybe somewhere at the back of our minds is the thought that we will be happy when we have enough money, or our children start behaving themselves, or we find the right partner. We'll be happy when we get through this difficult period and things sort themselves out. Well, it could be a long wait.

Or perhaps you notice yourself thinking that you would be happy if things had worked out differently or you'd been a different person in the first place. That's a convincing line of thought because just believing it makes it likely to come true. But what would happen if we let go of our ideas about our lives so we could really live them?

Another part of the answer is that, being natural, happiness grows when the conditions are right. You can't make a flower grow, but if you plant a seed in the right soil, give it enough light and ensure it has the water it requires, it will develop bit by bit, and the little brown speck you started with will sprout and spread and finally bloom. In other words, you can't make yourself happy, but you can foster the conditions that encourage happiness to arise.

William Blake put all this much better than I can in his little poem:

'He who bends to himself a joy

Doth the winged life destroy.

But he who kisses a joy as it flies

Lives in eternity's sunrise.'

The kind, funny and touching reflections in this book teach us how to notice when we bend joys towards us, trying too hard to make life how we want it to be, rather than letting it fly. It doesn't ask us to grasp the moment or seize the day, but rather to 'kiss a joy as it flies', opening to the beauty and love that's all around us, and then letting it go again. Follow the book and you'll learn to practice appreciation, generosity, acceptance, spaciousness and awareness. How else can we become engaged and open-hearted; and how else can we be happy?

It's something to learn – a day at a time and one thought at a time. And the time to start is right now.

Vishvapani Blomfeld, Writer and teacher of Buddhism and Mindfulness

Reviews

What do people say about this book?

'A great book! I find it a wonderful manual to carry with me as I journey through the year. I like the fact that the entries are brief and practical and can be read in a few minutes. Each entry introduces a simple topic and finishes with a practical application we can use throughout the day. Highly recommended.'

Eamonn O'Brien, MCAHyp, DABCH, Counsellor & Advanced Hypnotherapist

'I thoroughly enjoyed The Happiness Book, for it's quirkiness, simplicity, and thought provoking effect. Being a busy person, as most of us are these days, it was great to be able to dip in, from day to day, not only for inspiration, but really to think about my life, in ways that often get missed in a busy schedule. While striving for the next goal, Jo enabled me to stop and discover the happiness I'd been missing, along the way. It's a book I shall be revisiting on a regular basis. Thanks, Jo.'

Greg Forde, Director, Leonidas Business Consulting Ltd;
Principal, The Atkinson-Ball College;
President, The Corporation of Advanced Hypnotherapy

'By following the daily reminders in this book, you'll be guided to stay on track throughout the year, continuing to become more aware of your thoughts and attitude, make positive changes where necessary, and develop more appreciation, gratitude and happiness in your life!'

Toni Mackenzie, Best-selling author of 'Your Flight to Happiness:
A 7-Step Journey to Emotional Freedom'

Introduction

Hello there, how are you?

Welcome to The Happiness Club. My name is Jo Howarth
and I am so glad that you made the decision to buy this book.
I truly hope that it helps you to choose happiness every single
day of your life from now on.

I set The Happiness Club up in April 2015 after I realised that,
through my work with individual clients and in running workshops,
what I was helping people to find was their own happiness.
I knew from personal experience that happiness can be hard
to hold on to and I wanted to find a way to help people choose
happiness every day.

And so the club was born. My members receive a thought, tool or
technique every single day of the year to remind them about the
important things in life, to give them a nudge about ways in which
they can be happy, to help them see the good in any situation.

This book is a compilation of those thoughts that I've shared with
my clubbers over 180 days.

So how do you use it?

Well, you can sit down and read it from cover to cover like
a regular book.

Or you can read one page each morning in the order they
are given and use the information for that day.

Or you can close your eyes, put your trust in the universe, flick
the pages until you stop at a random point and read the thought
for that day.

Or you can do all three. *It's entirely up to you*, it's your book.

Hellooo and welcome!

Congratulations on your decision to read this book

...and to allow yourself to receive happiness every day!

That, rather obviously, forms the basis for my happiness thought of the day – the ability to greet all new experiences with open arms.

We have a choice as to how we receive new experiences and respond to them. Every experience, big or small, good or bad, carries the potential to teach us something.

If you approach each day with that in mind, then it will help you to embrace whatever happens. Personally, I would rather greet things with a smile. It simply feels better than the alternative.

So I hope that you greet this new experience with a smile and keep that smile in place *all day!*

My notes about this page: ○ Read it   ○ Liked it

Hello there!

I have a **question** for you today

"Are you pleased to be here?"

I don't mean here at The Happiness Club (I already know you're pleased about that!), I mean here, on this planet, in this life?

If the answer is no, then just take five minutes right now, close your eyes and think of all the good things you have in your life.

If the answer is yes, then just take five minutes right now, close your eyes and think of all the good things you have in your life.

No folks, that isn't a typo, whatever the answer is I want you to do that quick and simple exercise. Remind yourself of all the *amazing things* that are in your life and then hold on to them during your day.

My notes about this page: O Read it   O Liked it

....

....

....

....

Hi there, and how are you today?

Do you follow your **instincts**?

I was in the kitchen recently, making a family breakfast.

I opened the cupboard to get glasses out for our orange juice. As soon as I opened the cupboard door, a spider, medium sized, jumped out and onto the work top. And I mean jumped, properly jumped, it didn't fall, it jumped. This made me jump. Obviously. And then it didn't move. It just sat there. This struck me as odd. So I got a glass out of another cupboard and, very bravely I think, popped it over the top of the spider. It still didn't react. I then went to get my hero husband. He came, looked and said it was just a normal spider but I asked him to check so he Googled it. Turns out it was a Mouse Spider, which in the UK is not massively dangerous, but it can bite and the bite can hurt. Mr Mouse Spider is now enjoying himself at the very far end of our garden courtesy of my husband. All good.

The point of this story, for me, is about instinct. I knew there was something odd about this spider. Obviously the jumping thing was weird to start with, the way it sat there and didn't move, the way it looked etc. All of these things alerted something in me. My lovely husband tried to reassure me that it was fine and normal, but I knew there was something not right about it.

A few years ago, I would have allowed myself to be reassured by someone else, I would have quashed whatever my instinct was telling me in favour of someone else's opinion. But that day, I listened to my instinct. I listened to that inner voice. I listened to myself.

Do you?

My notes about this page: ○ Read it   ○ Liked it

Hello, I hope all is well in your world.

Hands up if you think you are **compassionate**?

...now, hands up if you think you are kind?

Hands up if you are compassionate and kind to other people?

Hands up if you are compassionate and kind to yourself?

It's a brilliant thing to be kind to other people. It helps to make someone else's day brighter and better and it gives you a lovely boost of wellbeing. All good stuff. But very often we are nicer to others than we are to ourselves.

So today, be kind to yourself. If you make a mistake, tell yourself it's okay, it's only human. If you do something 'wrong', forgive yourself and learn from it. If you're feeling a bit down then be gentle with yourself, give yourself a hug. Find someone else to give you a hug, speak softly to yourself.

Be kind to *you*.

My notes about this page: ○ Read it   ○ Liked it

....

....

....

....

How are you today?

So who here takes time **every single day** to relax?

Relaxation is a vital part of your health and wellbeing on the path to happiness.

However, most of us fill our time with busy-ness, doing things, making sure things are done, writing lists of things to do, thinking up new things to do. We don't have time to sit down and do nothing for 15 minutes every day!

Do we?

Give it a go today. *Plan* in some relaxation time, at a time that suits you. Do something for 15 minutes, just 15 minutes, that you find relaxing. Read a book, have a bath, meditate, sit down, whatever the thing is do it.

And... *relaaax...*

My notes about this page: ○ Read it   ○ Liked it

Hello there.

Would you like **more money**?

Quite often people hold the belief that with more money they would be happy.

With more money they could have the house they want, the car they want, the possessions they want, the holidays they want, belong to the clubs they want and go to the places they want. And all of those things will then make them happy. Yes, financial freedom is a good aspiration, but it doesn't in itself bring happiness.

True happiness lives inside us; learn how to be happy with what you already have and the world is your oyster.

So today, don't focus on the lack in your life, accept where you are and appreciate what you *do* have.

My notes about this page: ○ Read it   ○ Liked it

....

....

....

Hello, how is life treating you today?

How well do you know your **neighbours**?

Do you smile and wave at each other every day?

Do you know their names? Do you know their children's names? Do they have pets? What are their hobbies? What are their jobs?

If you can answer all those questions, hoorah you are obviously connected nicely with the people in your immediate environment. If you can't, then why not take a little time today to smile broadly and start a chat.

Connect with the people around you, it'll give you both a nice, warm, fuzzy feeling inside.

My notes about this page: ○ Read it   ○ Liked it

Hey up clubbers.

Home is where the **heart** is

What a wonderful saying – a clever person came up with that one.

Home is the place where we can absolutely be ourselves, kick our shoes off, breathe a sigh of relief and relax. Home is the place where the people we hold most dear in the world also live. Home is the place where love lives. It is where the heart is.

Keep that thought in mind today and take time to appreciate your home and the people in it, even if that is just you.

Take time to tell them that you *love* them.

My notes about this page: ○ Read it   ○ Liked it

....

....

....

....

Hello there.

Today I want you to imagine that it is Sunday evening

You have had the weekend off to rest and relax, get those much needed jobs done and have time to yourself.

Now, project yourself forward to the evening before you return to work. How do you feel? This is a perfect time to take a step back and view your working life.

Take a moment and ask yourself: Does your work fulfil you?

Does the idea of going to your work fill you with a warm feeling every day?

Are you passionate about what you do?

Does it make you happy? *Should* it?

My notes about this page: ○ Read it   ○ Liked it

Hi, how are you?

Today I simply want you to **repeat** the following phrase

Do it as many times as you possibly can and notice how you feel every time you say it:

"I allow myself to smile and feel happy."

My notes about this page: ○ Read it   ○ Liked it

....

....

....

Hellooo.

Stop what you are doing and **find a window**

Look out of the window and see what you can see.

Notice the colours, see the shapes, pay attention to whatever is happening and see the energy in the world around you.

Whether your view is a beautiful landscape or a brick wall, find something beautiful in it and give it your attention.

My notes about this page: ○ Read it   ○ Liked it

Greetings!

You are a **unique and special** being

Don't you believe me?

Did you question it? Did you laugh when you read that? Or did you think it was a bit over the top of me to say it?

Those reactions come from the beliefs that are stored in your subconscious mind. They are beliefs about yourself and about the world around you.

I promise you that you are a unique, special and beautiful being – there, I added one more in! And I promise you that I will do my best to help you come to *believe* that about yourself.

My notes about this page: ○ Read it   ○ Liked it

....

....

....

....

Hello again.

Practise this next time you are **driving somewhere**

Tell yourself that when you get to your destination there will be a parking space waiting and ready for you.

If your destination has a car park then a space will be available, if it doesn't then you will find somewhere to park nearby easily.

Spend the journey telling yourself this convincingly and repeatedly at intervals. I do this all the time, generally a space is waiting or has just become available when I arrive, and the longest I've ever had to wait is ten seconds.

Give it a go and *see*.

My notes about this page: ○ Read it   ○ Liked it

Hello, how are you?

Did you **find a parking space** without a problem yesterday?

Great isn't it?

The only time it doesn't work is if you allow doubt to creep in. If you think to yourself 'this is silly, it won't work' then guess what? It won't work! If you truly believe and expect a parking space to be there, then it will be.

Now imagine if you used the power of that belief and expectation in other areas of your life. What could you possibly achieve if you simply had *faith*?

My notes about this page: ○ Read it   ○ Liked it

Hello, hello, hello!

Today I want you to think about how you **talk to yourself**

What kinds of things do you call yourself?

Silly? Stupid? Forgetful? Clumsy? Naughty? Bad? Pay attention today to the words you use to describe you, make a note of them if it helps, and notice if you use one or more words regularly.

My favourite for myself at the moment is to call myself a 'doofus' when I forget something or make a mistake. Do I really think I'm a doofus? Nope. Consciously I know I am an intelligent, articulate,

strong and independent woman. Subconsciously, there is a belief in there that I am stupid on some level and I know where that belief comes from. Believe me, calling myself a doofus is an enormous step up from what I used to call myself.

So pay attention today to those words and see if you can find a softer or more positive way to describe yourself.

My notes about this page: O Read it   O Liked it

How's it going today?

What words did you **notice** that you use about yourself?

Were they good ones?

Wouldn't it be better if they were?

A little challenge for you today:
I want you to send a message or
a text to five people that you know
and ask them to describe you in
five words.

Then notice any differences between
the words you use for yourself and
the words that others use for you.

"Go!"

My notes about this page: ○ Read it   ○ Liked it

....

....

....

....

Hello there.

How do you **feel** about the passing years?

There were quite a lot of 'big' birthdays in my family in 2015

My mum turned 70, both my brother-in-law and sister-in-law turned 50 and our nephew turned 21.

So it got me wondering how you feel about age.

Do you hide your head under the pillow and check the mirror for wrinkles, or do you value the experience that life gives you?

Do you dread reaching those milestone ages, or do you embrace the changes that come with them?

Do you groan with each passing birthday, or do you take the opportunity to celebrate the fact that you are alive?

Which version of each question sounds *better*?

My notes about this page: ○ Read it   ○ Liked it

Helloooo.

My lovely husband and I went on
a grown-up night out recently

We had a lovely time with family, eating good food and having a boogie.

I spent a portion of the evening watching people dancing and it really brought home to me the power of music. Every person on the dance floor was having fun with lovely big smiles on their faces. It was truly delightful to watch.

As I watched further, I noticed that some people were completely involved in what they were doing, letting themselves be free and expressing themselves wholeheartedly. Whilst others were a little self-conscious, holding themselves back to varying degrees, still smiling but more reticent.

So, how do you dance?

Do you care what other people are thinking? Do you hold yourself back? Does it matter what you look like?

Or do you dare to feel the rhythm and go with the flow? To feel that freedom and elation and allow it to take over?

How do *you* dance in life?

My notes about this page: ○ Read it   ○ Liked it

....

....

....

Hi, how are you?

Right, today I'm talking about **grumpiness**

"What?!" I hear you exclaim, "this is supposed to be The *Happiness* Club!"

Yes, yes I know, but sometimes to focus on what you want, it's necessary to focus first on what you don't want.

So, what makes you grumpy? For me, it's a lack of food. My family are all the same and my lovely husband can tell when I'm hungry simply by my mood change! I noticed it most recently on a family trip to London.

Towards the end of one of our days out, looking for somewhere to get some dinner, I could feel my mood slipping. Similarly, as we left the restaurant having eaten our fill, I checked in with myself again and noticed how much my mood had lifted. I needed food, I got grumpy; I got food, I got happy.

So take some time and identify what makes you grumpy and use that knowledge to identify what would make you happy.

Then do that. *All the time.*

My notes about this page: ○ Read it   ○ Liked it

Good day lovely people.

Aren't there an awful lot of **close-minded** people out there?

I was reminded of this fact recently, via a debate on Facebook.

People who only believe something if it has been proved and double-proved to them. Or people who can only believe in something if somebody else provides them with rock-hard evidence. The debate began because somebody decried something that I believe in. They dismissed it on the grounds that there was no scientific evidence for it. They dismissed it without ever having tried it for themselves.

Now, obviously, I'm not here to judge the way that other people think, that is entirely up to them. But, what happened during this debate was that these people kept trying to make me wrong. I didn't fit into their view of the world, therefore I must be wrong.

And obviously I don't believe that I am wrong, I believe that I am entitled to my opinion as much as anybody else. I also believe that unless you have experienced something for yourself, then you have very little right to dismiss it. And so the debate rolled on for most of the day.

So there are two messages in here for you today:

Do not let somebody else's opinion make you wrong. It is simply their opinion and you are entitled to yours, allow yourself that.

And also thank you, thank you for being open to the world and to this new experience. Congratulate yourself right now for being open-minded enough to embrace something *new* in your life.

My notes about this page: ○ Read it ○ Liked it

Hello!

Today I'm **going back** to my recent grown up night out

Some real classics were played, songs that I remember from my childhood and beyond.

It was a 70s tribute night and so the music was obviously fab. Many of the songs were those I danced to in cheesy nightclubs as a student. There were a few that stood out for me:

'I Will Survive' by Gloria Gaynor took me straight back to being about 22 when myself and a group of my drama student buddies took our own show to the Edinburgh Festival. Just listening to that song brought back so many good memories of the fun we had.

A few songs later the DJ put on 'Dancing Queen' by Abba. I'm sure this song brings back all kinds of memories for everyone. For me, it is the one song that I would get up and dance to in a club with my two best friends at University. When I was younger, I never felt comfortable dancing, way too self-conscious. But this song would always get me up for a boogie. It became our anthem for the next 20 years or so and listening to it that night took me straight back to the heart of those friendships and put the biggest smile on my face.

The power of music and its association, huh?

So clubbers, your task today is to find a piece of music that uplifts you, that feeds your soul, that puts that big smile on your face, that gets your blood pumping, that puts you on a high. And play it as *often* as you can.

My notes about this page: ○ Read it   ○ Liked it

Hello again and how are you?

Today I want to know your answer to **this question**

Do you always do your best?

Actually, do you know what? I already know the answer.

The answer is

yes! **yes!** yes!
yes! yes!

Always. Without fail. We all do the best we can every single day.

Sometimes you might feel like that best isn't good enough, for yourself or for the people around you. But whatever situation you are in, rest assured that you are doing your best.

For where you are right now in your life you are absolutely 100 per cent doing your best, I promise.

So how about recognising that fact today and cutting yourself just the *tiniest* bit of slack?

My notes about this page: ○ Read it   ○ Liked it

....

....

....

....

Hey up clubbers!

Now then, on Day 22 I asked you if you **always do your best**

Today I'm going to expand that thought:

If you always do your best, then it also means that everyone around you is always doing their best too. I struggled for a long time with this side of the equation. Certain things happened to me in the past that meant I couldn't conceive how the people involved had ever been doing their best.

Eventually my mist cleared and I realised that this statement is true of everyone. We are all doing our best, every single day, given where we have come from, what we have experienced and the point that we are at in our lives.

So in the same way as I asked you to cut yourself some slack, have a go at cutting the people around you some slack. Whether it's someone close to you or someone you hardly know, whoever you come into contact with today bear in mind that they are doing their *best*.

My notes about this page: ○ Read it   ○ Liked it

How are you today?

We've talked over the last couple of days
about **people doing their best**

So the next logical step is to start looking at judgment.

I used to be incredibly judgmental; I would criticise what someone was wearing, how they looked, what they did, what they said etc, etc. I wasn't really aware that I was doing it, it was a normal, natural part of life for me.

The people who know me have heard me talk about my mentor and how much he has taught me over the years. Gradually, with his guidance, I began to realise what I was doing. By judging other people, I was actually judging myself.

The things that I picked out in others were the things I was unsure of or disliked about me.

So, have a think and pay attention to your thoughts and words today.

Do you judge others?

What kind of things do you think or say?

And is that *really* what you think of yourself?

My notes about this page: ○ Read it   ○ Liked it

....

....

....

....

Hellooo.

I'm going to talk about **trust** today

Specifically, trust in the flow of life.

There is a definite flow in life, a flow that we are either in or not. That flow is the process of life, the stream of life if you will. Think of a time when everything in your life ran smoothly, without hiccups. That time might have lasted for a few minutes, days, weeks or even longer. However long it lasted at that time, you were in the flow, going with it smoothly.

That flow is possible for all of us to achieve all of the time, it's just that our limiting beliefs, negative emotions and general baggage get in the way and make it hard sometimes.

So today, I want you to put your trust in the process of life, trust that life is unfolding as it is meant to and that the flow will carry you with it.

Just for today tell yourself, *"I trust the flow of life"*.

My notes about this page: ○ Read it   ○ Liked it

....

....

....

....

Hi there.

I've had an **amazing** few days

I ran a Happiness Workshop which was ace.

The prep for it went smoothly, and the event flew by and felt like the most natural thing in the world for me to do. Then I got my little family ready and we drove to deepest, darkest Somerset to celebrate my mum's 70th birthday. It has been lovely to see my mum, my brother, sister and their families. We spent the evening celebrating with old family friends. As I sit in our hotel room now, I am looking forward to a leisurely morning and Sunday lunch before we drive back up the M5.

What a lovely, lovely time.

In the past, these days would have looked very different. I would have panicked about my prep, forgetting things, doing things quickly, feeling anxious. I would not have been confident about my ability to run a workshop, I would have been nervous and second guessing myself. I would have spent the workshop wondering if people were enjoying it and then hours afterwards criticising myself and my performance.

I would have dreaded travelling south on a Friday evening and I would have been nervous about allowing those old family patterns of behaviour to affect me.

There are many reasons why there is such a difference between the two scenarios. The main reason is quite simply my inner attitude. I told myself that my workshop would be ace, that I would be awesome and that I would easily be ready in time. I told myself that this weekend was going to be brilliant fun. I expected these things to happen and they did.

So today, think of a situation you have coming up, tell yourself how amazing it is going to be, how brilliantly you are going to act, how ace you are going to be. Truly expect it and it *will* happen.

My notes about this page: ○ Read it ○ Liked it

Hello all and how are you today?

I spent most of my childhood **outside** in the countryside

Today I'm going to ask you all to take 10 minutes today, just 10 minutes, and go outside.

If you have a garden go there, or go for a 10-minute walk. In that 10 minutes I want you to really focus your attention on your environment.

Pay attention to all the beautiful things around you – see what you can see and see it in detail, pay attention to the detail. Have a sit down, close your eyes and hear

what you can hear. Then focus on what you can smell. Touch things. Use all of your senses to be fully present for those ten minutes.

Take a deep breath of fresh air and allow yourself to feel *refreshed* and *rejuvenated* by your connection with nature.

My notes about this page: ○ Read it   ○ Liked it

Hey clubbers, how are you?

Today it's all about **control**....

How much do you like to be in control?

How much do you *need* to be in control?

How much do you feel in control?

How much are you in control?

Which aspects of your life do you feel like you have control over and which don't you?

Wow, that's a lot of questions, huh? Ask yourself them all, maybe jot down the answers.

Then....

What if I told you that you are *always* in control? And that actually the more you let go, the more in control you are. Sounds backwards right?

And yet it is true. Have a go today at *letting go* and see what happens...

My notes about this page: ○ Read it   ○ Liked it

Greetings!

Hands up if you've got enough **time**?

Do you have plenty of time to do everything you want to do? All the time in the world?

We all have very busy lives, rushing about all over the place, squidging things into our diaries until they are fit to burst. Further down the line I am going to teach you a few techniques to help you manage that time better. But for now I am not going to tell you to lessen your load or tell you off for the bursting diary and lecture you about how you need to adjust your priorities.

Nice aren't I?

Nope, I am going to suggest a very simple attitude adjustment, because when we cram our lives full of things to do, we cram our heads full of things to remember as well. We put ourselves into a panic that we're going to miss something or forget to do something or run out of time to finish it all. So today I want you to tell yourself "there is time for everything I want to do". Make that statement with conviction *every* time you start worrying about the jobs left on your list and see what happens in your brain.

My notes about this page: O Read it   O Liked it

Hello all!

Following on from my recent thoughts on time and control, today I am thinking about **pressure**

Specifically, the source of pressure.

We very often get wound up or stressed about tasks we haven't yet completed or situations we can't control. Have a little ponder and see if you can trace back to the original source of the pressure you are feeling. Who put you under that pressure? Was it you?

For instance, one of the things that I used to get very wound up about was being late, late for school, late for meetings, late to meet friends, late, late, late. It's something I'm still working on for myself but I am about 90 per cent better than I used to be. One of the main reasons that I have improved is because I came to the realisation that the person who was putting me under pressure to be on time was me. Yes, okay, the girls have to be at school at 8:50 but actually the world is not going to end if they are five minutes late.

And by putting myself (and thus them) under pressure to be there before 8:50, I was making our mornings into a bit of a whirlwind, getting grumpy and cross with them and generally creating an atmosphere. Once I realised that I was the source of my own pressure, I could let it go. And once I let it go, everything became calmer. We leave the house these days largely on time and in a much calmer fashion, hoorah!

So who puts you under pressure to get a certain job done or to be in a certain place at a certain time? *Is it you?*

My notes about this page: ○ Read it   ○ Liked it

....

....

....

....

Welcome!

This is being written on the first day of a brand
new month, a chance to **start afresh**

Well actually, every day is a chance to start afresh.

But the start of a new month feels
like a good time to make a conscious
decision to do that doesn't it?

Some very wise people once told
me that in order to start afresh,
you first have to acknowledge
where you are. Acknowledge
and accept where you are in
your life, physically, emotionally,
spiritually, geographically, mentally,
behaviourally, career-ily (okay I
might have made that word up).

Accept where you are in every area
of your life. Once you have done that,
it is so much easier to look forward
and start afresh.

So wherever you are in your life at
this moment in time, tell yourself
"I am where I am and that's okay".
This is your mantra for today.

My notes about this page: O Read it   O Liked it

Hi there!

So yesterday I asked you all to **acknowledge**
where you are, right now, in your life

To acknowledge it and accept it.

Allow yourself the grace to be exactly where you are and to realise that it is okay.

We spend our lives looking forward, planning and fretting and wondering and dreaming about where we want to get to. Absolutely nothing wrong with having an idea of where we want to be. But sometimes we can get disheartened if things don't happen quickly enough, a bit like kids on a long car journey "are we there yet?" and "how much longer will it take?"

So today I'm going to ask you to take a look backwards. Take yourself back five years and make a mental note of all the things you have achieved in that time. You might still have work to do, things you want to achieve: we all do but take a few moments just to recognise how far you have come. And then give yourself a *big* pat on the back.

My notes about this page: O Read it   O Liked it

Hellooooo.

Thank you. Thank you. Thank you. Thank you. **Thank you.**

This is what I want you to do today.

Every time something happens to you today I want you to say thank you. Whether it's a good thing or a bad thing, if someone says something good to you or something bad to you. Whatever happens to you today, say thank you.

Every single thing happens for a reason, I truly believe that, and every single thing can teach us something.

So open yourself up to that learning today and the simplest way to do that is to say thank you. You'll find that with this attitude, even the *bad stuff* feels okay.

My notes about this page: O Read it   O Liked it

Hi again.

Do you know? Yesterday I was a **right grumpy** old fart.

I know, hard to believe, huh?!

Well believe it or not I do get grumpy. We've discussed before that one of my triggers for grumpiness is a lack of food but yesterday was down to a lack of sleep. My hobby is to sing with a 20-piece swing band and we had a gig on Saturday night. Normally when I get home from a gig I wind down with a cup of tea and a chat with my lovely husband for an hour or so. But on Saturday, I was so tired when I got in that I went straight to bed.

I didn't have a good sleep, tossing and turning all night. Thus I was tired and somewhat grumpy on Sunday morning. It reminded me how important sleep is in our pursuit of happiness. The key thing that

I forgot to do on Saturday night was to give my brain time to wind down properly. I went to bed with the excitement and nerves from the gig still whirring around my head. So even though I was physically tired, mentally I was still up and grooving.

So if you have trouble getting to sleep or staying asleep in the night make sure you give your brain proper wind down time. Do something relaxing for half an hour or so before bed. For instance: light reading or TV (not 'War & Peace' or a horror film!), a warm bath, meditation or simply do nothing at all. Do something to prepare your brain and get the *best* out of your sleeping time.

My notes about this page: O Read it   O Liked it

Hey up clubbers!

When you read this, I would like you to take two minutes and **close your eyes**.

Now imagine that you live in a world where you can be, do or have absolutely anything you want.

You can be exactly the kind of person you want to be, you can do all those things that you want to do, you can have that car or that house or whatever it is you would like.

Then open your eyes. How did that feel? Good?

Do that exercise regularly and you'll be doing two things:

1) Giving yourself a lovely shot of happy feelings

2) Telling your subconscious mind what you want your reality to look like

And then your subconscious mind's job is to make that reality true.

Cool, huh?

My notes about this page: O Read it   O Liked it

Hello folks

As I sat down to write this morning's thought
I had absolutely no idea what I was going to write.

**There's honesty for you, not one single clue
what my fingers were going to type.**

Have you had moments like that? Where you know you have to do something but you don't know what exactly it will be or how to start?

When you feel like that, what is your response inside? Panic? Anxiety? Confusion? Frustration? Not so long ago I probably would have responded with all of those!

When we allow those negative emotions to take charge and cloud our minds, then it simply makes what we have to do even harder. Our brains actually cannot operate properly if panic or anxiety take hold.

So next time you find yourself in a situation where you have no idea what to do, close your eyes, take a deep breath, calm yourself down, put your trust in the universe and yourself, tell yourself that the right thing will happen and *see* what unfolds.

My notes about this page: ○ Read it   ○ Liked it

Hello, hello, hello!

A simple one for you to **mull over** today.

What is life?

Life is not what happens after work,
life is not what happens in the
evenings or at the weekends, life
is not what you do when you're on
holiday, life doesn't begin when you
retire. Life is every single minute, life
is now, life is everything you do all
the time.

Enjoy!

My notes about this page: O Read it   O Liked it

Good day all

How does it make you feel when **other people succeed**?

If someone you worked with got that big promotion or a competitor got that lovely big contract, how would you feel?

If someone you know won some money or a holiday somewhere exotic, what would you think?

Very often we turn in on ourselves when other people do well, the thoughts that go through our minds can be very negative. We may feel like that person doesn't deserve that good thing, that life is unfair, that our lives would be significantly improved if we were the lucky one instead. How we wish something good would happen to us. We may even feel emotions such as jealousy, frustration and resentment.

My job today is to let you know, without a shadow of a doubt, that there is enough for all of us. Enough happiness, enough love, enough money, enough opportunity, enough success, enough joy. Whatever you want, there is enough of it in the world. I promise.

So next time something good happens to someone around you, have a go at feeling genuinely happy for them and you'll see how much better that makes *you* feel too.

My notes about this page: O Read it   O Liked it

....

....

....

....

Happy day everyone!

Have you noticed how children live entirely in **the moment**?

They do exactly what they want and go with how they are feeling every single minute of the day.

One minute they are having a cry then something distracts them and they're off exploring, then something makes them laugh and they're happy, then another distraction and they're busy making something. They don't expend valuable energy worrying about money, housework, bills, jobs, etc.

Today, have a go at being more like a child. Immerse yourself in each moment of the day, go with how you feel and do what feels best to you. Catch those thoughts about money or things you 'have' to do and put them to the back of your mind, just for today. *Enjoy yourself.*

My notes about this page: ○ Read it   ○ Liked it

Greetings all!

A bit of **light relief** for you today.

Enjoy doing this...

Next time you find yourself feeling a bit bleurgh or down or anxious or anything negative, I want you to try this:

Smile.

Wow, that sounds a bit simple, huh?

Have a go though. It works. There is an incredibly close connection between body and mind that works both ways. So physically make yourself smile and psychologically it makes you feel better.

Cool, huh?

My notes about this page: ○ Read it   ○ Liked it

....

....

....

....

Good day you lovely person.

Today I'm going to give you a **live demonstration** of how this gratitude thing works.

I have been working on the content of this book for six months or so now.

I'm writing something new every day and I feel incredibly lucky to have the opportunity to do this and blessed that people are interested in reading it all.

So today I'm simply saying thank you to you: thank you for being part of this book, thank you for coming on this journey with me. I am getting so much out of doing this and I truly hope you are too. Each one of you is an amazing person that I am sincerely pleased to interact with in this way. Thank you.

Feels good huh? Hold on to that today.

My notes about this page: ○ Read it   ○ Liked it

Hello all!

Do you like **hugs**?

Silly question, who doesn't?!

Do you like hugs? Silly question, who doesn't?!

But did you know it's actually good for you to hug? A hug is a great way to get oxytocin into your system and oxytocin helps to calm your nervous system, lower blood pressure and boost positive emotions. Cool, huh?

So today I want you to give out hugs left, right and centre: the longer the better and the more the merrier!

Enjoy!

My notes about this page:　　　　　　　　○ Read it　　○ Liked it

....

....

....

....

Hello one and all!

Do you know something? I've been doing **too much**.

I know that because for the last few days I haven't been well.

I don't get ill very often these days and I put that down to my largely healthy lifestyle and mindset.

So, when I do catch a bug I know that it is my body's way of telling myself to slow down and take it easy. So that's what I'm doing. I cancelled most of my work yesterday and all of it for today.

I'm listening to myself and today I want to invite you to do the same – what is your body trying to tell you? Are you listening? Or do you soldier on in the belief that other people's wants and needs are more important than your own?

Have a go at putting yourself *first*....

My notes about this page: O Read it   O Liked it

Hello, hello! How the devil are you?

Can you tell I'm feeling **better** than I did on day 43?

Amazing what a good rest can do isn't it?

I encourage you all to take one.

The best bit about feeling ill is feeling better. This morning I find myself appreciating everything even more than usual; I have spent a couple of days feeling rubbish and now that I feel more like myself it's like I've been supercharged. I have had a reminder, a solid experience, of how life feels when I'm not completely healthy and it has made me so thankful for my health.

So my thought for today is that sometimes we all need to experience things we don't want in order to fully appreciate the things we *do* want.

My notes about this page: ○ Read it   ○ Liked it

....

....

....

....

Happy day everyone!

I spoke to someone on the phone a couple of days ago

It was a friend I haven't known for very long.

In the space of a 20-minute phone call this person told me about five mutual friends that they didn't like and why. There was not a good word to be said about anybody else that came up in the course of the conversation. To be frank, it made me feel sorry for the people that were being talked about and for the person saying these things.

It got me thinking. We've talked before about how we talk about ourselves and about judging other people. But what kind of things do you say about others?

Your challenge today is to bite your tongue if you feel something negative about someone else is about to come out. Find something good to say instead; *it feels better.*

My notes about this page: ○ Read it   ○ Liked it

Hello there!

Today I'm going to ask you to take a moment
and **close your eyes**.

I want you to imagine that you have reached a ripe old age.

You are on your death bed but you are perfectly happy and content with that fact and with the life that you have lived.

As you lie there, waiting to go on to whatever happens next, you are reflecting back over your long and happy life. Thinking about all the things you experienced and achieved. Imagine if you reached 100 years old for instance what direction your life could take and the things you could achieve. Take a few minutes to do this exercise and notice what things from this life stand out as key moments, key people, key incidents. From a happy and content perspective: what did you do, who did you love, where did you go, what did you experience that really gave you happiness?

Hold on to those thoughts today.

My notes about this page: ○ Read it   ○ Liked it

Hellooo there!

Today I'm thinking about doing things
that you **don't really want to do**.

But, no, I'm not talking about the washing up or the housework here.

I'm talking about the kind of thing that you feel obligated to do, out of a sense of wanting to make someone else happy or not wanting to let someone down.

Just take a moment to think of a situation like that, where you have felt like you have to say yes to something.

Now, while you're thinking of that situation just check in with yourself emotionally, how does saying yes

to that thing make you feel? A bit squirmy maybe? Uncomfortable? Ill at ease? Something stronger?

It's lovely to do things to make other people feel good but often we do them at the expense of our own feelings. It can be hard to start with but learning to respect your own feelings and say no allows you to take a step forward on that path of happiness.

Look after *you*.

My notes about this page: ○ Read it   ○ Liked it

Hey up clubbers.

The post today is a short one
and your quest **sounds simple.**

Just for today make the choice not to believe your thoughts.

They are just thoughts, they are not
true, they do not have to be reality,
they are just thoughts.

Every time you catch yourself
thinking something today ask
yourself "do I know this to be
absolutely 100 per cent true?"

You might *surprise yourself* with
the answers.

My notes about this page: ○ Read it   ○ Liked it

Welcome to today!

I did just want to take a moment to remind you
all these daily thoughts are meant as **a guide** for you

They are things for you to ponder and have a go at.

They are not meant as absolute
instructions that you MUST do as
a reader of this book. If something
I suggest appeals to you and feels
right then do it, if it doesn't apply or
feels too difficult then be gentle with
yourself, allow yourself to participate
at your own pace.

In fact, apply that concept to your
whole day today.

Enjoy.

My notes about this page: ○ Read it   ○ Liked it

....

....

....

....

Hello, how are you?

I think mine must be one of the only professions in which it is considered a good thing to **make someone cry**.

We spend our lives bottling things up.

We push the negative feelings down inside of us and hold them there so we don't have to face up to them, using a lot of energy and headspace in the process. And it's understandable; negative emotions can be scary, they can represent scary things that may have happened.

I very much believe that allowing that energy to be released is the way forward. Now I'm not advocating endless rounds of sobbing for no reason, but what I am saying is that crying is okay. Crying indicates a shift of energy, a release of negative emotion, a move in the right direction.

If we turn towards our negative emotions, acknowledge them, allow them to come up and out, then we are freeing up energy for ourselves, energy that we can then put to positive use.

Keep that information in mind today, check in with yourself and if some negative emotion appears, then have a go at saying *hello*...

My notes about this page:　　　　　○ Read it　　○ Liked it

Hello there lovely people

Last weekend my family were **out and about**

We decided to visit a well known sandwich shop for our tea.

We went in to our local one; it was pretty much empty, there was no queue so we took our time to decide on what we would all like and then gave the lady our order. We stood there watching her put our sandwiches together and after a couple of minutes my daughter turned to me and said, "Why is she rushing mummy?"

To be honest I hadn't really noticed until my lovely girl brought it to my attention but the lady serving us was going at about a million miles an hour, cutting bread, putting ingredients on, toasting things and wrapping the sandwiches up. There was no queue, there was nobody behind us, there was nobody waiting. There was no reason for her to rush.

Her training was obviously to do everything as quickly as possible or maybe they had been so busy earlier she had just got into the habit of going quickly. But there was no reason for her to rush.

Are you getting the analogy yet, my lovelies? We spend our lives rushing around, getting stuff done, doing it quickly even when we don't necessarily need to. We are told throughout our lives, trained, to do things quickly and move on to the next thing. We get into the habit of rushing through life. Rushing when there is no need.

Take it *slow*....

My notes about this page: ○ Read it ○ Liked it

....

....

....

....

How are you today?

What was the **first thing** you did this morning?

What is the first thing you do every morning?

The alarm goes off, your eyes open and you .... (fill in the blank).

Do you wake up feeling groggy and moan at the thought of getting out of bed? Do you bound out of bed looking forward to what's coming? Are you somewhere in-between?

Whatever your usual reaction is to waking up and getting up I would like to invite you to try something different tomorrow.

As your eyes open, make a conscious effort to think of three things that make you smile and allow that smile to happen. You might not remember to do it every morning; cut yourself some slack and do it as often as you can.

In fact, do it now, when you've finished reading this.

It's a *much better* way to start the day.

My notes about this page:　　　　　　　　○ Read it　　○ Liked it

Happy day everyone!

Hands up if you remembered to think of three things that make you smile when you woke up this morning?

And don't put yourself under undue pressure...

...you don't have to try and think of something different every morning. My three things are largely the same every day.

I would like you to take a few moments now, as you read this, to think back over yesterday and identify anywhere that you feel that you made a mistake or could have done better or didn't quite behave the way you would have liked to. Got something?

Now, forgive yourself.

Do this every morning, as soon as you awake, while you're having your morning cuppa, in the shower, wherever it works for you.

Tell yourself that you are forgiven for any mistakes from yesterday; this is a new day and you are going to do *the best you can* today.

My notes about this page: ○ Read it   ○ Liked it

Hello one and all.

Will it be today **forever**?

Will this day go on and on ad infinitum?

Will everything always stay exactly the way it is today?

Or will time move on until a brand new day dawns?

My wish for you all today is that you recognise and accept that everything is temporary. Time moves on, circumstances change, new things happen, feelings change.

If now is a wonderful time for you, realise that it won't always be and allow yourself to appreciate it fully. If now is a rubbish time for you, realise that it won't always be and allow yourself to feel hope for what is coming.

Take care.

My notes about this page: ○ Read it   ○ Liked it

....

....

....

....

Hi there!

Is there something in your life that you are trying to do at the moment?

Are you trying to do it or are you doing it?

There is an enormous difference between "trying" and "doing". An attitude of trying implies that we can't do it, that what we want to do is insurmountable, that we are bound to come up against obstacles that will stop us.

An attitude of doing means that no matter what happens we will get there, that we can overcome obstacles, that we intend to reach that goal whatever happens along the way and however long it takes.

So I will ask you again: are you *trying* to do something or are you doing it?

My notes about this page: O Read it   O Liked it

Hey up folks!

I'd like you to imagine that you have **been on holiday** for a few days.

Today is your first day back at work.

What was your reaction to that thought? Did you groan a bit, wish you didn't have to go and feel a bit unwilling? Or were you excited to get back to forging ahead with that side of your life?

Now imagine that your boss rang and offered you a couple more days off.

How do you feel now? Elated that you don't have to face work for

a while longer? Or are you looking forward to going back to work after some more 'you' time?

I want you to take a few moments to ponder your reaction, realise how much of your life is spent at work, how many minutes and hours you spend doing your job.

How would you *like* to feel about it?

My notes about this page: ○ Read it   ○ Liked it

Hi! Hope your world is fun today.

Hands up if you are **holding a grudge** at the moment?

Or if you have ever held a grudge against someone?

It could be something from long ago or more recent, it might be something that had a major impact on your life or something smaller that just niggles away at you.

If someone has wronged you, it is so easy to hold on to those negative feelings, to direct your hurt, frustration, anger, resentment at someone specific.

I would like to invite you to recognise that those negative feelings are mostly affecting one person. You. Holding on to negative feelings uses a whole lot of energy up. Energy that could be used in a more positive way.

So now, take a deep breath in and as you exhale I want you to consciously decide to let that grudge go. Tell yourself that you will allow yourself to release whatever the negative emotion is inside you about that thing. Breathe it out.

Feel *lighter*?

My notes about this page: O Read it   O Liked it

Well hello there.

I spent the day with **my gorgeous family** yesterday

We messed about at home and then went to a park in the afternoon.

The girls were playing on swings, monkey bars, climbing walls, etc. As I was watching them I noticed how my youngest daughter always let her big sister go on things first and watched very carefully so that she knew what she had to do when it was her turn. She didn't ask anyone how to do something, she simply watched and learnt from her sister.

Now my eldest daughter didn't necessarily know what to do either, she was watching the children in front of her as well but my youngest assumed that her big sister was right.

It reminded me that this is how we all learn when we are children; we learn how to do things, how to behave, how to respond, how to think, how to express ourselves – all by watching the bigger people around us.

But remember, just like my eldest daughter, those big people we were watching didn't necessarily know what they were doing, we simply *assumed* they were right.

My notes about this page: ◯ Read it   ◯ Liked it

....

....

....

....

Hello folks!

I'm going **back to the park** in my post today

My eldest daughter has a bit of an obsession with the monkey bars.

She's been attempting to master them for about a year now. To start with, she could just about hang on to the first one before dropping to the ground. Gradually she managed to swing to the second one before dropping and so on.

It's taken a while. She has experienced various emotions throughout her monkey bar journey, frustration, fear, anger and jubilation to name but a few. She has never given up and we have encouraged her, praised her efforts and assured her that she absolutely can do it. Whenever we go to a park, the first thing she asks is if there are monkey bars there and can she go on them. They are the first thing she runs to and has a go on. She has been utterly determined to master them.

A little while ago we went to the park and suddenly she managed to swing all the way across, no fuss, no nonsense. She was so pleased with herself, it had finally all clicked into place; she got her technique right and it now works every time.

Let me summarise the analogy for you: if there is something you want, keep going, allow yourself to experience all the emotions involved, learn from them, be determined, tell yourself how well you are doing. It might take longer than you think but believe you can get there.

You can.

My notes about this page: ○ Read it   ○ Liked it

Hi there!

I had **a gig** with the Big Band last night

Two things happened which I thought made rather a nice thought for today.

This is a long one folks, make yourselves comfy!

One of my songs in the second set was a song called 'At Last'. Some of you may know it. It's one of my favourite songs ever. I sang it at my mum's wedding and I used to sing it to my eldest daughter when she was a baby, it has big emotional connections for me. I thought that I sang it okay, but to be honest I thought it was a bit ropey; I had a few duff notes in there, it was passable but definitely not the best I've ever sung it. In the interval a man came over to where I was sitting, looked at me and said, "At Last? Amazing." I was utterly taken aback and said to him, "Wow, thanks, I thought it was a bit ropey to be honest!" He tapped his chest and said, "No, it was amazing, got me right here." You honestly could have knocked me down with a feather.

A little later on during one of the instrumental songs, there was a guitar solo; the songs we play don't often have guitar solos so it was good to listen to.

I thought to myself that I wished I could play an instrument that well, to have put the hours of practice in, to master an instrument in that way, it sounded great. During the interval I found myself standing at the bar next to the guitarist; he was shaking his head and berating himself for messing up the solo, he had missed notes, he had played wrong notes, etc. I told him, honestly, that I hadn't noticed any of that, I thought the solo sounded lovely and I wished I could play the guitar like him.

Both of these things made me think about how different our internal view of something can be compared to what the people around us see. We judge ourselves so harshly sometimes, we berate ourselves, we believe that we're not as good as we can be, we're not doing something well and that the people around us must think the same. But very often those around us are seeing and feeling something completely different, *remember that.*

My notes about this page: ◯ Read it   ◯ Liked it

....

....

....

....

Hellooo!

Amongst other things I am a **Reiki practitioner**

Reiki has a list of ideals for us to work to and I wanted to share one of those with you.

The ideals are cleverly written as they ask you to do something "just for today" not to put pressure on yourself to always do something, but to do it "just for today". So the ideal I want to share with you is: Just for today, I let go my anger.

Have a go at saying this to yourself; catch yourself today every time you feel irritation or frustration or anger building up in you about something. Tell yourself that just for today you will let that emotion go, just let it drain back out of you, don't hold it in, just let it go.

Just for today.

My notes about this page: O Read it   O Liked it

How is your day so far?

My message is **simple** today

We listened to The Beatles whilst driving around in our car yesterday.

The song that resonated most with me was, "All you need is love, all you need is love, all you need is love, love, love is all you need".

In the evening we watched the final of Britain's Got Talent. I was attempting to do some work at the same time. After a week off, I had quite a few emails to catch up on so thought I would use that time to do it. Halfway through the programme, my beautiful youngest daughter came and asked me to sit and cuddle her. Because of that song, I chose love over work.

The girls went to bed very late last night and it was my turn to cuddle them in bed. To start with, I couldn't get the fact that I still had work to do out of my mind. Eventually, because of that song and a conversation with my beautiful husband, I chose love and stayed with my girls 'til they were both fast asleep. The work has been rearranged in my diary, there's always time to catch up another day. The evening was a great reminder for me of the most important thing in the world, love.

So today, I encourage you to *choose love* whenever you can; when you have a choice to make today, choose the one that gives you love.

My notes about this page: ○ Read it   ○ Liked it

....

....

....

....

Helloooo!

How often do you say to yourself "I **want** that"
or "I **wish** I had this"?

As humans, we do this all the time.

We talk and think about things we want, the things we wish we had in our lives, the things we are lacking.

When we "want" something, what we are doing is focusing our attention on the lack of it, if we want it then we don't have it. We are reminding ourselves that we don't have it. Does that make us feel good? Nope.

Today when you get one of those "I want" thoughts, take a moment to imagine, just pretend, that you already have that thing. Allow yourself to experience how good that feels.

Now *hold on* to that feeling.

My notes about this page: O Read it   O Liked it

The sun is shining, hooray!

I need your **help** please.

I'm on a drive to sell this book.

I think a few testimonials from existing readers would help me convince other people to buy it. I would be so grateful if any of you would write me a couple of lines saying what you like about the book and what you get out of it? Thanks.

Now then, hands up if your opinion of me has changed because I asked for your help? Hands up if you think less of me because I need a bit of a hand? Or are you happy to help? Do you like being asked to help?

Very often we are more than happy to help others when they need it, actually it helps to give us a sense of achievement and it boosts our wellbeing because we feel good about ourselves. But we tend to hang back or shy away from asking for help ourselves.

Today I would like you all to focus on help – giving it *and* asking for it. Open up and ask those around you to give you a hand; you might be surprised at the reaction you get.

My notes about this page: O Read it   O Liked it

Hello there, how are you today?

I'm a bit **tired** this morning

My hubby and I went out last night and I'm up early to go and run a workshop at a local school.

Feeling tired has brought my mind to thinking about sleep.

I wrote a while ago about the importance of getting enough sleep in order to boost your wellbeing. Sleep is nature's healer, it is the time when your brain and body repair and recharge themselves.

So for those of you who may have trouble getting enough sleep, here is another top tip. Reduce the amount of electrical items in your bedroom. Our bodies have their own natural electric stimulus – it's what keeps our hearts beating and our brains working. This natural flow can be affected by the electrical flow of the devices we keep around us, even if they are on standby.

One of the worst offenders is... can you guess? Our mobile phones. Oh no, I hear you cry, she's going to tell us we're not allowed our phones in the bedroom!

Nope, don't worry, if you do sleep with your phone next to you, then I am simply going to advise you to switch your phone to Airplane mode before you go to sleep. That simple switch stops your phone emitting a signal to communicate with the Wi-Fi network, a signal which can interfere with your sleep patterns.

Anyone who knows me knows that I love sleep. Getting enough good quality sleep helps you to be more relaxed, it improves your memory, helps to regulate weight and generally makes you healthier. If sleep is something you struggle with then have a go at getting rid of the electrical stuff in the bedroom and make that simple switch on your phone.

Take care of you.

My notes about this page: ○ Read it   ○ Liked it

Happy sunny day everyone!

Actions speak **louder** than words

They really do.

How many times have you heard someone talking the talk without walking the walk? How many times have you done that too? We all have.

It can be so easy to talk about what's important, what we want to achieve, what we want to do, etc. But very often our actions don't back up what we're saying and we make excuses as to why that is. "I would do it if I had enough time", "I would if I could", "I'd love to but I have to do this other thing first". And so on.

Actually if you're honest with yourself you know that you are making excuses, that for some reason you are avoiding the thing that you say you want. And that doesn't feel good inside. Does it?

Today, why not have a go at backing yourself up. Have a think about something you want, have a think about what actions you would need to take to achieve it and then take one small step towards it.

Be gentle with yourself; it doesn't have to be huge but do something that gets you nearer to it. Then pay attention to how much *better* that feels inside.

My notes about this page: ○ Read it   ○ Liked it

Hi, how are you?

"Whether you think you **can** or you think you **can't,** you're **right**"

That was Henry Ford. He was a clever old bean wasn't he?

I'm sure there are things in your life that you believe you *can* do. Let's use a simple example: we can all make a cup of tea if we want to. We know we can do that. There is no doubt in our mind that this task is possible, do-able (is that a real word?!), achievable. In fact, we're so assured in our ability to make a cup of tea that it doesn't even enter our heads to question that ability. Pay attention for a second to that feeling of complete confidence and belief.

Now, on the flip side of that quote, if you think you can't do something then guess what? Chances are you can't. How many things are there in your life that you tell yourself you can't do?

Have a go today at taking that 'cup of tea feeling' and *applying* it to something that you normally tell yourself you can't do.

My notes about this page: ○ Read it   ○ Liked it

Helloooo.

I took my youngest daughter
to a **birthday party** yesterday afternoon

it was very cute, lots of five-year-olds running around, dancing and generally having fun, hooray.

One of the games they played was along the lines of musical statues except when the music stopped, the kids had to do an impression of whatever the entertainer said. He was quite funny shouting out things like "helicopter" and "washing machine" as well as easier things like "butterfly".

As I sat and watched, I noticed that most of the kids did the same actions as each other for most of the impressions. There were, however, one or two kids who stood out because they did something different to everyone else. The interesting thing was that generally those kids swapped to doing the same as the others as soon as they noticed that they were different.

It got me thinking again about how we learn, how we copy those around us so that we can belong to the pack, being the same as everyone else feels safer and that's not necessarily wrong.

But there was a part of me that wanted to stand up and cheer those different kids on, to tell them that it was okay to do things your own way, that to have the confidence to stand out and be yourself is amazing.

Just a thought.

My notes about this page: ○ Read it   ○ Liked it

Hello there!

I'm going back to the **Reiki Ideals** again today

There are five of them in total and they are all incredibly simple yet incredibly wise.

The one I'm going to share with you today is, "I show kindness to all living things".

We've touched on kindness before and we will doubtless touch on it many more times. Kindness is a key component of happiness, kindness to other people, kindness to yourself, kindness to *all* living things.

I used to be the kind of person who wouldn't think twice about squishing an ant or treading on a spider. Whether I was willing to admit it at the time that was mostly out of a vague kind of fear or dislike for little creepy crawly things. Then I was taught the Ideals, and gradually I realised that life is life. My decision as a big human being to squish something littler than me was not a good one.

Now I go out of my way to keep everything alive. Tissues and glasses and pieces of paper are employed to move ants and bugs and spiders, to allow them to continue on their journey safely. Because who am I to decide that something doesn't deserve to live in safety, just because I am bigger and have the ability to squish them?

Keep that in mind today, don't squish things that are smaller than you, whether it's a bug or a person.

Thanks.

My notes about this page: ○ Read it   ○ Liked it

Hey up clubbers!

Love yourself

Give yourself some love.

Direct that love inwards.

Love you.

Love, love, love, love, love, love, love.

There's nothing more important.

Close your eyes, think of whatever
you need to in order to bring up
a feeling of love. Now direct that
feeling of love to yourself.

Do this as *many times* as humanly
possible today.

My notes about this page: ○ Read it   ○ Liked it

Good day clubbers!

Last night as I was putting my onesie on, my **leg** got caught up

---

You know those ribbon loops that are put inside clothes to hang them up with?

No idea what they're called. Anyway, my onesie has really long ones inside and I always get my foot caught in them when I put them on. Always. And it annoys me. Every time.

Last night I got my entire leg caught up in the ribbon. Once again I tutted and felt that vague annoyance pass through me as for the millionth time I said to myself, "I really must cut these things out".

And then I stopped and realised that I really must cut these things out. I've been saying it for months, literally months, without doing anything about it. So I got my scissors and cut the blinking things out.

No more getting my feet and legs caught, no more annoyance, no more mild frustration. Just relief and pleasure knowing that it won't happen again.

I'm going to encourage you all today to do the same thing. I don't mean cut the ribbon loops out of your clothes (unless you want to), I mean actually *do* that thing that you always say you are going to do. That thing that if you do it you know you will feel better but for some reason you are always putting off.

Don't put up with the frustration and annoyance, let yourself experience the *relief* and *pleasure*.

My notes about this page: ○ Read it   ○ Liked it

Happy day everyone!

I used to be a **Corporate Event Manager**

It's quite a stressful job with lots of deadlines.

I was very good at making "to do" lists in order to get all the necessary jobs done. The problem was I would feel the weight of those lists. For instance, it's Friday today so I would have taken time to get jobs finished off and then work out what I was going to need to do next week and make lists ready for that.

It gave me a feeling of being organised and ready, which was great. But it also brought home to me how busy next week was going to be. I would mull over that all weekend in the back of my mind and I would dread going to work on Monday because I already thought it was going to be a busy, hard week.

I still make "to do" lists and I plan my diary in advance so that I am organised and ready. The difference these days is that once I have planned my work in, I let it go out of my head. I take each day as it comes.

Sometimes I genuinely don't know what I'm doing tomorrow, I know that my diary will tell me so there's no need to panic but my attention is fully on what I'm doing today. I treat each day as an entirely new entity instead of lumping all the work I have to do in a week together and looking at it all as one big, huge, looming thing and dreading it.

So that's my thought for you today – today I'm suggesting that you treat each day separately.

Let some of that *weight* go.

My notes about this page: O Read it   O Liked it

....

....

....

....

Hello, hope you're well.

I'm late this morning: my family are usually
fairly lazy at the weekends

So, we got up late and I cooked a bacon and pancake breakfast which we have just finished eating, yum.

Halfway through cooking breakfast, I felt quite anxious.

I started feeling anxious and instinctively I tried to ignore it and carry on cooking. I tried to ignore it and burnt the pancakes. I tried to ignore it and forgot to put the kettle on. I tried to ignore it and was grumpy with my girls when they came into the kitchen playing.

And then I caught myself trying to ignore it and realised that I needed to follow my own advice. So I turned towards it, I acknowledged it, I recognised where in my body I was feeling that anxiety. I asked myself what thoughts were going through my mind when I started feeling anxious. I paid attention to that feeling.

And I realised that I felt anxious because I was late and I knew I was going to be late writing this page and getting on with my day. Being late is one of my stress triggers, even though ironically I am often late (still got some work to do there I guess!)

The next time my girls came into the kitchen, I gave them hugs and kisses. My lovely husband came in to help and I asked him for a hug too. My point is that by paying attention to the feeling, by recognising it and acknowledging its presence I was able to do something about it. Ignoring it simply made it worse, amplified it, changed my behaviour.

So today have a go at simply acknowledging how you feel at *any* given moment, pay attention.

My notes about this page: O Read it   O Liked it

Greetings one and all!

So today, I'm writing this page to you all from **Bristol**

I'm running a resilience workshop at a school here this afternoon.

I travelled down to Bristol yesterday afternoon and stayed at my sister's house last night. The journey from door to door is about 170 miles and it usually takes about three hours.

Yesterday it took me over four hours to get here. The traffic on the M6 was heavy and slow and at times it was hard going. Sometimes I didn't move at all and sometimes I had to divert off from my planned route.

But I knew I would get here, it didn't cross my mind to question whether I could make the journey from Rainhill to Bristol. Even when I had to leave my planned route I knew what my destination was, that never changed. I knew I would get here eventually, even if it took a little longer than I thought. At no point did I think "oh I'll just turn round now and go home, Bristol is an impossible place to reach, I can't do it".

I knew if I kept moving in the right direction that I would reach Bristol at some point.

We all have goals in life, things we're working towards, things we are trying to achieve. But we allow ourselves to be disheartened by difficulties, sidetracked by distractions and put off by obstacles. We start to believe that we can't do it, we can't get there, it's impossible.

Next time you feel like that, I want you to remember my journey to Bristol. Hold on to the belief that whatever happens along the way, eventually you *will* get there.

My notes about this page:　　　　　　　○ Read it　　○ Liked it

Helloooooo!

An **early start** for me today, which got me thinking about time

Aren't we all slaves to it?

We live our lives by the clock, running here and there to be on time for everything, it's awfully important in our world to be on time for everything.

Last summer when my family went on holiday, I decided on the first day to take my watch off. Partly so it didn't get ruined on the beach, and partly as an experiment to see how I would react. I was expecting to feel a bit lost and a bit twitchy without it, but actually it was incredibly liberating. To know that I could just go with the flow of the day, eat when I felt hungry, drink when I felt thirsty, do whatever I felt like doing when I felt like doing it. I loved it.

When we came home, I put my watch back on because I told myself that I couldn't live as though I was on holiday all the time. But it

really didn't feel right on my wrist anymore. I went back to constantly checking what time it was, checking if I was going to be late, checking if I was on time, checking what time it was, checking what time it was... checking, checking, checking.

So about a month after our holiday I took it off again and to this day I have not put it back on. Best thing I ever did. There is always a way of finding out what time it is if I need to. I've confessed before that I have a tendency to be late; wearing a watch didn't stop that, it simply made me more anxious about it. My attitude to time has relaxed enormously, I don't feel the need to constantly check anymore, I don't feel beholden to it. Simply because I took my watch off.

Take *yours* off today?

My notes about this page: ○ Read it   ○ Liked it

Good day lovely people!

I'm going back today to the **birthday party** I took my youngest daughter to a couple of weeks ago

The entertainer was quite good.

He was largely a DJ who played games that involved stopping the music and having the children do something. So, games like musical bumps, musical statues etc.

As I sat and watched it became apparent that he only ever chose a winner for each game. When the music stopped he didn't pick out the child who sat down last and make them 'out', he just said how well everyone was doing, how hard it was going to be to pick a winner and then started the music again. At the end of the song he would ummm and ahhh and then pick a winner out of all the kids. And he was careful to pick a different child every time.

At first this approach bemused me, but the more I watched the more I liked it. None of the kids ever felt like a loser, they might not win the game but they weren't singled out as the worst one either. And they pretty much all got to win one of the games.

Good, huh? Imagine how much better that feels, to recognise that you aren't the best at one thing but you are at another, to recognise that not being the best doesn't make you a 'loser', it just means you didn't win this time. Adopt that attitude next time you're facing something hard. If it doesn't work out, it's not the end of the world.

If you don't win this time, it doesn't mean you're a loser it just means you might win the *next* one.

My notes about this page: O Read it   O Liked it

Greetings everyone!

This afternoon **I am speaking** at a conference

Well, actually I'm on a Q&A panel.

I have literally no idea what to expect; I can't prepare anything because I have no idea what questions will be asked. I have no clue as to what the other panelists' views are on life, the universe and everything and I have no idea who will be attending.

I'm excited. Years ago I would have been petrified, being put on the spot and having to come up with an answer would have sent me into nervous, fearful spasms. I would have run a million miles from it. Today I'm excited to find out what happens, I'm looking forward to seeing what other people say and to telling them my truth.

Does the 'unknown factor' stop you from doing things? If you're unsure exactly what might happen, do you shy away from trying something?

Can I tell you a secret? Everything is unknown until it happens. Everything.

There are things you can plan for, there are things you are used to doing so often that there is an expectation of what will happen but actually everything is unknown until it happens.

How great is that? You face the unknown countless times every single day and you survive. *Ace.*

My notes about this page: ○ Read it   ○ Liked it

Hi how are you?

As you know I was **on a panel** at a conference yesterday

It was an interesting, fun experience.

At one point the person running the conference asked me a specific question about my personal story. We were over-running on time by that point and when I was halfway through my answer they sped me up. I managed to get one of my messages across but a key point about forgiveness was missed before it was time to move on to another speaker.

I have had a slightly twitchy feeling ever since and I realised this morning that it is because I wasn't allowed to finish. I didn't get to put the full stop on my story and I didn't get to share something that might have helped somebody.

So today if someone talks to you, listen. Give them your attention. Don't cut them off, don't speed them up. Don't stop them because *you* think they have made their point. Allow them to tell *their* story until they reach the full stop.

My notes about this page: O Read it   O Liked it

Hello!

I've got **backache**, a fairly persistent pain
in my lower back

It's mostly from lifting and carrying small children.

They are actually too big for me to carry but I can't resist the cuddles!

Do you look after your body? Happiness comes from physical wellbeing as well as mental and emotional. So how much attention do you pay to your body and whatever it is trying to tell you?

When you've got five minutes today have a go at this:

Sit on a chair, shuffle your bum to the back of the chair, have your feet flat on the floor and your hands nice and loose in your lap. Close your eyes to allow yourself to focus inwardly. Now, pay attention to how your feet feel against the floor, does it feel solid or something different? How does the floor feel against your feet?

Now move up your body and simply pay attention to each part of your body in the same way. How does your body feel in the places where it connects with the chair? How does your body feel in the places where it connects with itself? How do your legs feel? How does your back feel? How do your arms feel? Your neck? Your head? Your face? Are there any places where you can feel an ache or a twinge?

There's no right or wrong to this, it's simply about paying attention to your physical being. Just notice whatever you notice.

Enjoy.

My notes about this page: ○ Read it   ○ Liked it

Hello clubbers!

Everywhere I go at the moment I hear people giving advice about surrounding yourself with **positive people**

Believe it or not, I don't agree.

Getting rid of the naysayers in your life, leaving the negative people behind, etc. It has been playing on my mind for a while now, gently ticking over at the back there.

Yes, obviously it is easier to be positive and to focus on the positive yourself if all the people around you are positive too. But how possible is it to actually get rid of all the negative people in your life? I know there are people in my life that err on the negative side, that sometimes have to be coaxed round to seeing the positive. And they are not necessarily people that I can just dump or drop, they are people that I care about regardless.

What I am striving to help you all do is to reach that point where you are secure enough in your positivity and your sense of self that the negative stuff just washes off you. In that way you will not only be able to help yourself be positive regardless of the situation you find yourself in, but you will also be able to help those 'naysayers' see things a little differently too.

So today (and always) when you rub up against something negative I want you to say to yourself, "I am amazing" and keep repeating that phrase until you literally feel the effect of it inside.

Enjoy.

My notes about this page: O Read it   O Liked it

Hello again!

I have a **story** for you today

Two monks are walking through the countryside...

...in silence and in harmony with the beauty of the world around them. They come to a river and notice a beautiful woman standing by the riverbank. She is dressed in a fine dress, with expensive shoes and her hair and make-up is perfect. But she is upset.

The elder monk goes over to her and asks what is the matter. She replies that she is on her way to a wedding but her horse has bolted. She has arrived at the river and cannot work out how to get to the other side without ruining her beautiful shoes and dress. The elder monk offers to carry her across the river and she agrees in delight.

So the monk picks her up and gently carries her across the river, sets her down on the other side and wishes her well. The two monks continue their journey for a while in silence. The elder monk enjoys the beautiful countryside once again but then notices that his companion is not himself.

"Is something wrong, my brother?" he asks.

The younger monk cannot contain his anger any more "Yes of course there is, we take very solemn vows and we are expected to live by them. We have taken a vow of celibacy yet not only did you touch that woman, you *carried* her! How could you do that?!"

The elder monk smiles at his friend and says, "But I put her down on the river bank, why are you still carrying her?"

Good story, huh? Imagine what delights the younger monk missed along their journey because his focus was on what had happened in the past...

My notes about this page: ○ Read it   ○ Liked it

Hellooooo!

Every weekend, my family goes **swimming** together

We all have a swim in the main pool, and the girls also have swimming lessons.

Last weekend my youngest daughter informed me that she can swim now, and then she asked why she still needed to have lessons.

It's a good question isn't it? She's learnt the basics, she can float, she can kick her legs, she can move her arms, she can put her head in the water, she can get most of the way across the pool in one go. She can swim. That's good enough isn't it?

I explained to her that if she kept the lessons up, then she would get better and better at swimming, she would learn exciting new ways to swim, she would get more confident, and she would improve.

The conversation made me think about the way we live our lives. We can do the basics can't we? We can move, we can talk, we can think, we can work, we think to ourselves, "oh well, I'm kind of happy some of the time, that'll do", or "I can muddle through life feeling like this".

That's good enough isn't it?

Is it?

The way you get better at swimming is to learn, to practice and to keep practicing, to practice the same techniques over and over again until they become second nature to you.

So which of the techniques that I've taught you so far are *you* using every day?

My notes about this page: O Read it   O Liked it

....

....

....

....

Happy sunny morning everyone!

Once upon a time there were **three friends**...

They met at University and got to know each other very well.

They saw each other through hard times and good times. They helped each other through good relationships and bad. They stuck together through thick and thin. They watched each other get married and start families.
As their lives changed and grew, they naturally saw each other less and less.

This made one of the friends quite angry. She felt like she was putting in more effort than the other two; she expected them to make the same amount of effort. She expected them to be available to see her whenever she needed them, she expected them to live by the same high standards that she set for herself. She expected their friendship to be as important as when they had first met. She expected a lot.

Eventually this friend could stand it no more and she exploded; she told her friends that if they didn't make more effort then she no longer wanted to see them. She told her

friends that if she wasn't important enough in their lives, then she no longer wanted to see them.

Her friends told her how hard it was to be her friend, how her constant expectations were wearing them down, how her insistence on them being available made them not want to be available, how hard it was to live up to her expectations of them.

And so the three friends parted ways. The friend who had been angry now realised the pressure that she had put her friends and herself under for so many years, the pressure of expectation. And the force of that realisation allowed her to let it all go, to release her friends and herself, to be free.

What do you expect of the people around you?

What do you expect of yourself?

Can you let that expectation go?

(And yes, that angry friend was *me*)

My notes about this page: ○ Read it   ○ Liked it

....

....

....

Hi there.

I'm running a Happiness Workshop today and I'm **excited**!

When I was talking about the workshop this week someone said this to me:

"I don't know how you can stand up and do that, it must be so hard".

That comment got me thinking about how we view things and what we tell ourselves. Do you have things in your life that you think are hard? Things that you expect to be difficult, that you almost dread doing because you just know it's going to be hard? Things that before you do them you think to yourself "oh, this is going to be difficult, I'm not sure I can do this".

As you may know, I am a firm believer in the power of thought, the power of intention. If you spend minutes, hours, days or even weeks telling yourself something will be hard, then guess what? When you finally get around to doing that thing, it's really hard.

So now let's flip that on it's head. How do you think it might be if you spent minutes, hours, days or even weeks telling yourself that something will be easy?

Have a go.

My notes about this page: O Read it   O Liked it

Happy day everyone!

Does this sound **familiar**?

"Why isn't anything changing?"

"I want things to change, I know what I want and where I want to be but nothing changes, I don't understand why nothing is changing."

Do you get up at the same time every day?

Get in the shower, get dressed, have breakfast in the same order?

Go to work at the same time, along the same route every day?

Have the same interactions with the same people you see at work?

Get frustrated by the same things every day?

Come home again and do roughly the same things each evening?

Are you doing anything differently?

Do you change your routine at all?

I wonder why nothing is changing....

Today think of one thing you could do differently, it can be something small and simple from your daily routine, just do it differently and notice how that feels. Then tomorrow try something else in a different way and so on... is it *really* possible to expect change if you do the same things?

My notes about this page: ○ Read it   ○ Liked it

....

....

....

....

Hello one and all.

We have some **pots of herbs**
on the windowsill of our kitchen

Yesterday I noticed that they were becoming rather overgrown.

I took them down, chopped the Chives and the Parsley and then proceeded to pick the Basil leaves.

After a few minutes of plucking Basil, I thought I was pretty much done. I had picked off the discoloured leaves and put them in one pile and I had picked off the good leaves and put them in another pile. Then the girls asked me for some help with their game, so I left the Basil plant on the side and went to help.

When I came back a few minutes later I noticed a whole clump of good leaves and a whole clump of discoloured leaves that I had missed the first time.

It made me think of the phrase about using a fresh pair of eyes. I had been so involved in my task the first time around that it had actually become hard to see what was in front of me. When I took a break and came back, I could see very clearly what I had missed before.

Give yourself the opportunity to see what you're doing with a fresh pair of eyes. Take a break from whatever situation, task or issue you are dealing with then come back and see what you *missed*.

My notes about this page: O Read it   O Liked it

Hello there how are you?

I have **another story** for you today

Once upon a time there was a lumberjack...

He was young, fit, healthy and strong. He was starting a new job and he was very excited, he was going to be the best lumberjack ever.

So he turned up for his first day of work bang on time and set himself a target of chopping down 10 trees. He worked hard all morning, took his lunch and worked hard all afternoon until clocking off time. He had chopped down nine trees so he was fairly pleased and promised himself that tomorrow he would chop down 10 trees.

So he showed up bright and early the next day, worked hard all morning, took half his lunch break, worked hard all afternoon and finished at clocking off time. He had chopped down eight trees. He was a little bemused by this but promised himself that tomorrow he would chop down 10 trees.

He went in early the next day and worked through his morning break, took ten minutes for lunch, worked through his afternoon break and finished half an hour after everyone else. He had chopped down seven trees. So now he was getting a bit annoyed but promised himself that he would chop down 10 trees tomorrow.

The next day he started an hour and a half earlier than the others, worked all day, didn't bother with breaks or lunch and finished an hour after everyone else. He had chopped down seven trees. And now he was getting angry. Why on earth was all his hard work not paying off?

Then he noticed another lumberjack, twice his age, sitting in the sunshine enjoying a cool drink so he decided to go and talk to him.

"Can I ask you a question?" said the young lumberjack.

"Of course my son, how can I help?"

"How many trees did you chop down today?"

The older lumberjack replied, "15, I always chop down 15 trees"

The young man couldn't take any more and he exploded in anger.

"15?! 15?!?! I came in an hour and a half before you, worked *all* day, didn't bother with lunch and finished an hour after you!! And all I've chopped down is seven trees! I'm half your age, twice as strong, fit and healthy!! I've seen you today and all you seem to do is take breaks!! What's that all about?!"

The older man smiled gently and said, "Ah, but those breaks are when I sharpen my axe."

I love this story. Breaks are incredibly important – yesterday I talked about giving yourself the opportunity to see things with fresh eyes. Taking a break is an important part of this but breaks are also the time when our brain gets the chance to refresh and re-energise.

If you keep going and going and going and going *you* will break, so take one instead.

Hey up clubbers

I had a **passenger** in my car the other day

She lives close by me and I was giving her a lift home.

As we turned up one of the main roads she said, "Oh I hate driving up here, it's so depressing."

I asked her why she thought that and she said, "Just look at it, brick walls, wooden fences half falling over, dilapidated flats, it's horrible."

Her answer took me somewhat by surprise. All of those things are there and they aren't the prettiest things to look at admittedly.

But I was surprised by her answer because on the other side of the road is a park, a big green space with trees, bushes of all different colours, pretty flowers in the flowerbeds, kids running around having fun, the sun was shining and it looked beautiful. But this lady had paid it absolutely no attention whatsoever. Her focus was completely on the side of the road that needs a make-over.

Today, let your focus be on the *beautiful* side of the road.

My notes about day 87:   O Read it   O Liked it

....

....

....

My notes about day 88:   O Read it   O Liked it

....

....

....

Hello there!

It was **sports day** at the girls' school yesterday afternoon

The sun was shining and the competition was on!

My eldest daughter was not looking forward to the space-hopper race. Let me tell you why.

She has long legs, and in last year's race, she was given a teeny tiny space-hopper which meant that literally every time she bounced, she fell off. It took her five times as long as everyone else to finish the race but do you know what? She never gave up. Every time she fell off, she got straight back on and tried again until she got to the finish. I have never been such a proud mummy, and I was at the finish line to scoop her up in my arms when she burst into tears because she thought she had done so badly.

So, this year she wasn't looking forward to doing the race, but proud Mummy moment number 35,768 happened when I was watching her at the start line. Every time one of the teachers tried to give her a small space-hopper, she refused it. She shook her head and passed it down the line until about 30 seconds before the start of the race, she was finally handed a large one. She didn't win the race yesterday, but she only fell off once and she gave me a big thumbs-up at the end.

Brilliant stuff. If you fall off, get back up and try again until you make it to the end. And then learn the lessons, remember what happened last time and do something else to give yourself a different result *and* a better feeling.

My notes about this page: ○ Read it   ○ Liked it

Good day all, hope you're well.

Today's post is short, sweet and **simple**

I would like you to take every opportunity you can to compliment other people.

Whether you know them or not, have a go at complimenting every person you come into contact with today.

If they smell nice, tell them. If they look nice, tell them. If you like their clothes, tell them. If you like their hair, tell them. If they have a nice smile, tell them. If they do a good job for you, tell them. If you walk past someone with a dog tell them how lovely their dog is, etc.

The compliment doesn't have to be earth shatteringly huge, something nice and simple is fine. Put a smile on other people's faces today and watch how that makes *your* smile grow too.

My notes about this page: ○ Read it   ○ Liked it

....

....

....

....

Hello my lovely clubbers

How many people did you compliment yesterday?

I am going back to sports day for today's post.

As we sat in the sun watching each race, I joined in as much as I could, shouting encouragement to all the children I know, especially my own, obviously. I'm sure you can all imagine but I am quite loud at things like this; I get very enthusiastic and quite excited. I love watching the kids do their best, love watching the expression on their faces and seeing their joy when they finish whether they have won or not.

Years ago I would have sat quietly at the back, keenly watching for my children and not paying much attention to any race they weren't in. I wouldn't have dared to shout out or whoop. I would just about have joined in with the clapping.

There are two differences in me.

Number 1 is that I no longer care what other people think – the me from years ago cared very deeply that other people might disapprove or think badly of me. Now I realise that if they do, then that says a whole lot more about them than it does about me.

Number 2 is that I immerse myself in the moment, in the experience. I allow myself to feel the emotions of excitement and joy. I get involved.

That is my wish for you today. Immerse yourself in whatever you are doing. Allow your natural, instinctive reaction to something joyful to come out. Shrug off that worry that other people might disapprove and give your joy a voice.

It feels *ace.*

My notes about this page: O Read it   O Liked it

Hellooo.

I wasn't **very mindful** yesterday

It happens, I'm a work in progress.

My eldest daughter wasn't very well so she stayed with me instead of going to school. I took her along to one of my networking meetings, then out for lunch and then we came home to do some admin work. For various reasons, I didn't finish all the work I needed to do before it was time to go and get my youngest daughter from school. So, when we got back home I explained that I needed a bit of time to finish off my work.

It was gorgeously sunny here yesterday and my daughters love nothing more than going outside in their swimming stuff, running through our water sprayer and paddling in their pool. I encouraged them both to go out and do just that but my youngest daughter wanted me to go with them. I promised that I would as soon as I'd finished my work. So they waited for me.

Obviously my work took longer than I had planned and an hour later we finally made it outside. The sun had disappeared. It was cloudy, overcast and just a little bit chilly. We lasted about 10 minutes out there. I had assumed the sun would stay all afternoon and I missed the opportunity.

There is a saying, "Make hay while the sun shines" and it popped into my head at that point yesterday. Quite simply I could have found another time to do my work and enjoyed that precious fun time with my girls. I am grateful for the reminder lesson; next time the sun is out I'll be the first one in the sprayer.

So today, if you're given the opportunity to do something that will give you joy, take it. *Grab it* with both hands, don't miss out.

My notes about this page:　　　　○ Read it　○ Liked it

Hello there!

Does it **matter**?

This is the question I want you to ask yourself every time something winds you up, stresses you out or annoys.

When I was 25, my dad passed away unexpectedly of a heart attack. He was 50, there were no signs, no symptoms and then he was gone. It had a profound effect on me and changed the course of my life completely.

I remember in the months following his death the thought which continuously popped into my head was, "It doesn't matter." Things that had annoyed me previously, silly things, no longer had any effect. Things that people said that would have wound me up before no longer bothered me. Grudges that I had held on to for years no longer mattered. Whenever I felt myself starting to feel irritated, stressed or angry, the thought that would pop into my head was, "it doesn't really matter." Against the backdrop of my dad's death, nothing else was important.

The whole thing gave me an invaluable insight into what was actually important in this life, I still had much to learn but I was on the right path.

So today, if you feel any negative emotion building up inside you, ask yourself, "Does this matter, does it *really* matter?" And if the answer is no, then breathe that negative energy out.

My notes about this page: O Read it   O Liked it

Hello clubbers, how are we today?

I had a bit of a **car crash** yesterday

It's okay, it was nothing serious.

A lady reversed into the front of my car in a car park. The noise was deafening, so much so that I got out of the car expecting to see the bonnet in a big crumpled mess. But there was hardly any noticeable damage, a bending of the bumper. They make cars of hardy stuff these days, huh?

My instinctive reaction was to jump out of the car and ask the lady quite harshly if she had checked her mirrors at all. But I gave myself a deep breath and a bit of headspace before I got out of the car. I'm glad I did, because she was quite distraught and very much in shock, bless her. We were both headed for the same children's party, so both had our daughters in our cars which added to that "what if?" feeling. We swapped details and went on to the party, which is a whole other story!

I had a simple choice to make once we had swapped our details: to let that incident cloud the rest of my day, or not.

In the past, I would have considered my day ruined by such an event. I would have mulled over the details, replaying it all in my head, worrying about what might happen now, how much it might cost, how long it might take to get the car fixed, whether the lady would admit liability as she did when it happened, and on and on.

I chose not to do any of those things. I chose to carry on with my day in a positive way. Cars are easily fixed and I have a sore shoulder, but it won't last forever, it will all get sorted out in the end, what will be will be.

Whatever happens today, remember that you have a choice as to how you let it affect you. Would you prefer a day with a big black cloud over it, *or* a day of sunshine?

My notes about this page: O Read it   O Liked it

Welcome to today folks.

When we are young children, we learn that there are things we need to **ask permission** for

---

"Can I go here?" "Can I do this?" "Can I have that?" and so on...

It's a natural part of growing up; most of us go through a rebellious stage during our teenage years, but then we find ourselves in the work environment with a boss, and those beliefs about asking for permission get reinforced again.

It's hard to shake those beliefs off. We go through life seeking permission from other people to reassure ourselves that what we are thinking, feeling and doing is right. Obviously when other people are involved in something you want to do, then they need to give their permission as well, but most of us still seek permission for ourselves.

When I first started seeing my hypnotherapist, Eamonn, I was very unsure of myself, insecure and quite frankly scared of a lot of things. I would sit and tell him how I felt, what I wanted to do and why I wanted to do it. With his words and support I very much felt like he was giving me permission to do and feel those things. So I would allow myself to feel how I felt and do what I needed to do. Because I had permission from someone else.

The truth is that Eamonn couldn't give me permission, he could advise, support and guide me, but the only person who could give me permission to feel how I felt was me.

Who do *you* need permission from?

My notes about this page: ○ Read it   ○ Liked it

....

....

....

....

Hello there!

I was **walking in the rain** with my girls the other day

My youngest daughter said to me
"It's a horrid day today, isn't it mummy?"

She was talking about the weather, in the way that we all talk about the weather, in the way that we decide it's a horrid day just because there is some rain. Does rain really make the day horrid? Does the sunshine really make the day good?

Nope. It is entirely possible for us to feel amazing on a rainy day and rubbish on a sunny day. The weather is just the weather, there is no "good" or "bad" in it, it just is.

Don't let today's rain affect your mood, *decide* to be happy regardless.

My notes about this page: ○ Read it   ○ Liked it

....

....

....

....

Hello clubbers!

I parked in a car park the other day
where the machine **only accepted coins**

Obviously, I only had a ten pound note on me. *Hmmmmm.*

As I looked around, I noticed a charity shop across the road and saw the opportunity to do some good at the same time as getting some change. I walked over and went in, had a quick look around, picked up a couple of things and went to the till.

The sum total of my spend was £2. When I gave the lady my ten pound note, she froze and stared at me, "do you not have any change?" came the question.

I apologised and explained that I was only buying something to get change for the car park. At which point she tutted and said something along the lines of "that car park is a pain, I've got almost no change left, people keep coming in and buying stuff just to get change for that car park, it's a nuisance being across the road from it." I didn't comment, took my things and my change and walked back over to the car park.

Now I can understand that if people just keep coming into the shop to get change for the car park then that must be a little wearing, but the fact remains that I would not have gone into the shop and bought anything at all if I hadn't needed the change. The charity shop was £2 up simply because I needed change. Imagine how much money the shop was making from all the other people who just wanted change. Now how GREAT does it feel to be across the road from the car park?!

I wish I had pointed this fact out to the lady behind the counter; I wish that I had helped her to see the positive side of being across the road from the car park, I wish that I had helped her flip the negative attitude into a positive one.

Instead, I am using the story to suggest to you that you try flipping things today. If there is something that continually annoys or irritates you, stop and take a look at it, find the positive angle to it, change your perspective on it.

Find the good stuff.

My notes about this page: O Read it   O Liked it

....

....

....

....

Hello and welcome to the day.

I have **a plan** for you today

Start from wherever you are.

Each moment of each day is utterly unique and of itself. You have total freedom to start each and every moment afresh, to make a choice in each moment as to how you want to feel.

It doesn't matter what has happened in the past, whether that past is 20 years ago, or just two minutes ago.

Don't focus your attention on things you feel you have done wrong in the past, don't let the past define you and your actions in the present.

Don't think that you have to do things in the same way because that's how you've always done it, or believe that it's too late to change something. It is never too late.

Start from wherever you are, *right now.*

My notes about this page:

○ Read it   ○ Liked it

Hellooo everyone!

The girls and I went to an **impromptu screening**
of a well known children's film last night with some friends

My friend's little girl was fiddling and pulling at one of her teeth which was obviously starting to wobble.

She is six, and they get very excited when one of their teeth is about to come out. She kept coming over to her mum asking her to help her wobble it and get it out. Her mum very sensibly told her not to force it, that the tooth would come out when it was good and ready.

It got me thinking. If you force a tooth out, it hurts a lot more than if you just let it happen. If you force a tooth out there is often a lot more blood and gore than if you just let it happen. If you force a tooth out before it's ready, then often it takes longer for everything to calm down properly.

And so it is with life.

If you keep fiddling and pushing and pulling at something that you want to happen, if you try to force a result out of a situation then very often, it hurts a lot more than if you just let it happen; there is more blood and gore than if you just let it happen and it can take longer to calm down than if you just let it happen.

The tooth will come out when the time is right, when it's good and ready.

Just let it *happen*.

Hi all!

I was at a **networking event** recently

Halfway through the event I felt the need to powder my nose, if you know what I mean.

While I was washing and drying my hands, I noticed a sign on the toilet wall. It went something along the lines of, "these toilets are cleaned and inspected regularly. Please inform a member of our management team if you have any complaints."

What struck me was the invitation to complain. I think this is something we have become used to in today's society. We are invited to give our opinion on a vast array of services, but more often than not, we are invited to complain if we are not happy with something.

How about when we're happy with something? When we walk in and the toilets are lovely, sparkling clean? When someone gives us good service? When a shop looks nice? When somewhere has a good atmosphere? When a place makes us feel welcome and looked after?

How many of us actually bother to give positive feedback?

Have a look around you today, wherever you go. If you notice something good tell the relevant person, if you get good service, tell the relevant person, if something makes you feel good, tell the relevant person.

Let's start inviting people to *compliment* rather than complain.

My notes about this page: O Read it   O Liked it

....

....

....

....

Hello everyone!

The **question** I would like you to have uppermost in your minds today (and every day) is...

"Which is more important?"

It's a very simple tool that I use as often as my mind remembers to.

For instance, if you are having a disagreement with someone, of any age, take a moment to check with yourself. "Which is more important, the fact that I love this person and want them to be happy, or that I win this argument?"

If you have children and find yourself getting frustrated or losing your cool with them, ask yourself, "Which is more important, the self-esteem of my child or that they do as I'm asking?"

If you have a difficult situation at work, take a moment to check, "Which is more important, my health and wellbeing, or that I get all this work finished asap?"

I'm hoping you can see that the answer in each case is a no brainer. Love, happiness, self-esteem, health and wellbeing – they win every time.

Ask that question folks. Then adjust behaviour accordingly.

Enjoy.

My notes about this page:　　　　　　　　　O Read it　　O Liked it

Good day folks.

Who is your **best friend**?

Is it your partner or an old school friend?

Maybe it's your mum or dad?

Or someone you've met quite recently?

This is the person who knows everything about you, it is the person who understands why you think like you do, who understands your little quirks. This person understands how you feel when you are happy, when you are sad, when you are angry. This person understands why you feel those things and what has happened to trigger them.

This person always has your best interests at heart; they want the absolute best for you in life, they want you to achieve whatever it is that you want to achieve. This person will always be with you, taking each step of the road with you. He/she cares deeply for you and wants you to be happy.

So who is your best friend?

Is it your partner? Your school friend? Your parent?

Nope.

This person is *you*.

You are your own best friend.

Treat yourself like that today.

My notes about this page: ○ Read it   ○ Liked it

....

....

....

....

Happy sunshine everyone!

Let me ask you a **question**

Do you want to be happy?

Are you all nodding? Are you all saying, "Yes, Jo!"?

Let me ask you another question. Do you want to be sad?

Are you all shaking your heads? Are you all saying, "No, Jo"?

You do know that you have the choice don't you?

You do know that either emotion is entirely within your grasp?

You do know that you are the only person who can make it happen?

You do know that you're in charge, don't you?

Let me ask you with some emphasis. Do you WANT to be happy?

Are you all nodding? Are you all shouting, "Yes, Jo!!"

Good. Now spend the day reminding yourself, "I *want* to be happy" and choose the things that make you feel good.

My notes about this page: ○ Read it   ○ Liked it

Hey up clubbers!

Today, I'm **expanding** on my thought from yesterday

Does your happiness depend on someone else?

Does it depend on whether your partner is in a good mood?

Or whether your children are behaving themselves?

Or whether the people you work with treat you properly?

Or whether your family relationships are good?

Who do you give that power to?

How refreshing would it be if you could say to other people, "you can't hurt me, only I can hurt me"?

Take some time today to notice how the behaviour of other people affects you and ask yourself why that is, what is it about their actions or words that annoy, frustrate or upset you?

How amazing would it be if your happiness simply depended on *you*?

My notes about this page: O Read it   O Liked it

....

....

....

....

Hey up folks, how are you today?

One of the common themes I come back to in these posts is **letting go of old stuff**.

I want you to cast your mind back to your favourite childhood toy

it might have been a doll or a teddy bear, something that comforted you when you were little and made you feel safe. Mine was a cuddly lamb that I rather imaginatively called "Lamby" and he went everywhere with me. I took him to my friends' houses, I took him on family day trips, I cuddled him at night, I watched TV with him, I took him everywhere.

Now just imagine for a moment how it would be if I still did that. What if I brought Lamby to one of my networking meetings or to visit my friends. Imagine if I asked Lamby for his opinion while I was in an important meeting or asked him to help me help a client.

Sounds absurd doesn't it?

Can you imagine my client's face if I consulted a stuffed toy during our session?

Can you picture the looks on the faces of my workshop delegates if I stopped to ask Lamby what he thought?

It would be a little odd carrying a symbol from my past around with me and constantly checking in with it wouldn't it?

But that is exactly what we do with our thoughts and feelings from the past. We carry them around with us everywhere we go, we check in with them continuously and adapt our behaviour accordingly.

Have a go today at seeing those old behaviours as if they were your old toy and put them down.

Leave them in the past *where they belong*.

My notes about this page: ○ Read it   ○ Liked it

Hello there one and all.

Grab yourself a **piece of paper** and take five minutes.

Now, write a list on that paper of all the things
within you and around you that you love.

Just a massive list of everything
and anything, big and small, that
you love. So for instance here's mine
for today:

I love me (very important to start
with this one folks!)

I love my husband.

I love my eldest daughter.

I love my youngest daughter.

I love my family.

I love my friends.

I love my life.

I love my world.

I love the sunshine.

I love my Happiness Club
and its members

I love my work.

I love my clients.

I love presenting workshops.

I love holidays.

I love my patience.

I love my joy.

I love my abundance.

I love my health.

I love my calm.

I love my home.

I love my car.

I love my time.

I love my happiness.

It takes a few minutes, just tune
yourself in to the things you love
and make a big list of them all. Do it
every morning, soon as you can after
you get up. Remind yourself of all
those *amazing* things, it makes you
feel wonderful!

My notes about this page: ○ Read it   ○ Liked it

Hi!

Recently I went to a networking group that I have visited a couple of times but **don't go to regularly**

The organiser had sent an email to say the venue had changed at the last minute to a pub up the road.

I actually arrived a few minutes early (which is unusual for me!) and as I pulled into the car park I was struck by the simply amazing view. The far end of the car park looked out over the most beautiful countryside, rolling green hills, fields of wheat, the sky stretching on and on for miles. It was breathtaking.

So I parked at the far end of the car park, facing that view and took ten minutes out to sit and appreciate it fully. In that ten minutes a number of cars pulled into the car park, some parked to the side, others parked in line with me. Every single one of the cars that parked in line with me reversed into the space so the back of their car was looking out onto that view. The people got out of their cars and went about their business, oblivious to the beauty around them.

That ten minutes made me 'late' for the start of the networking but it gave me a deep appreciation of the beauty in our world, it filled me with a feeling of peace and contentment, it reminded me how great it is to pay attention.

Don't be oblivious today folks, *find* the beauty around you.

My notes about this page: O Read it   O Liked it

....

....

....

....

Hello there, how are you?

I was a bit **grumpy** yesterday

I was tired after our day out on Saturday and a busy week before, squidging clients in before I go on holiday.

My eldest daughter is being a bit testing at the moment, she's seven and she likes to see how far she can push the boundaries.

Those two facts were not a good combination yesterday, and I spent too much of my time allowing her behaviour to affect my behaviour and telling her off. Then feeling bad for telling her off.

I have woken up this morning and forgiven myself for yesterday, I cannot change it but I can avoid repeating it. So I have set the intention today to be kind.

Whatever happens, today I will be kind, which is within my power.

Cast your mind back over yesterday. Was there anything you weren't happy about with regards to your own behaviour, thoughts or feelings? Use that information to set your intention for today, whether it is to be kinder, happier, more positive, more relaxed – whatever it is, set that intention now, say it out loud and make a commitment to it.

It's all about taking small steps in the right direction, every single day folks. Be *gentle* with yourselves.

My notes about this page: O Read it   O Liked it

Hellooo folks!

I went to **band rehearsal** last night

I haven't done any singing for a while so it was lovely to clear the old pipes out.

It was ace.

There is one song in particular that I adore singing, it really suits my voice and is slap bang in the middle of my range. I love it. There are songs, on the other hand, which I struggle with. They are not my style and some of them are on the high side for me.

I realised last night that I was holding myself back from fully singing the hard songs because I'm not comfortable with them.

And I realised that was a silly thing to do, to hold myself in because of doubt and worry about what others might think. So I let myself go and sang my little heart out.

And it occurred to me that all of that made quite a good point for you lot. Whether you are good at something or not, if you enjoy it and are passionate about it, give it your all, don't hold yourself back.

Go for it!

My notes about this page: ○ Read it   ○ Liked it

....

....

....

....

Hey up! How's your day?

At band rehearsal on Monday night we ran through a set of songs that I haven't sung for **well over a year**

There were about six of them in total.

As I stood waiting for the intro of each one to start, I had the same thought. "I'm not sure I can remember how this goes."

But with each song as it came to my turn to join in, the melody kicked in and I remembered, I remembered all the little bits of each song as if I'd sung it yesterday. After about the 4th one, I said to the Band Leader, "I've got that 'riding a bike' feeling with these songs – once you've learnt it you never forget it".

And then I realised that that is the magic of your subconscious mind folks, it's all in there, everything you've learnt, everything you've done, everything you know. It's all in there just waiting to be brought out; all you have to do is relax, trust yourself, and let it flow.

Simple.

My notes about this page: O Read it   O Liked it

Hi all!

I told you all earlier that I was a bit grumpy with my **gorgeous eldest daughter** recently

---

That evening at her bedtime, I apologised to her for my part in our difficult interaction.

I apologised for being grumpy and impatient with her. She put her arm around my neck and gave me a squeeze as she said, "Mummy I love you all the time, when you're lovely and even when you're grumpy, I know we all get grumpy sometimes, but I still love you always."

Not entirely sure how I managed not to cry, bless her heart.

Unconditional love is a gift that many of us take for granted. When you spend every day with the same people, it is easy to forget how much of a gift their love is. They love you throughout all your moods, good and bad.

Hold on to *that* knowledge today.

My notes about this page: ○ Read it   ○ Liked it

Hello!

Hands up if you have a pair of **really comfy** old jeans?

A pair that you really love wearing, they fit you perfectly,

You can move around in them easily, you know what tops go best with them, you know how to wear them. They've got the odd bit of fraying going on, the material is a bit worn, there's maybe the odd rip but they are comfortable.

Now think about buying a new pair of jeans. They look so much better than your old pair. There's no fraying, no rips, the material is smooth and perfect. But they feel a bit stiff, they're harder to get on than your old pair and you have to breathe in a bit to wear them. Whilst they look good and you know they are better for you, after a couple of hours it's getting a bit hard to hold your tummy in all the time, it's getting a bit hard to breathe in the new way.

So after a while you take the new jeans off and you slip that old pair back on. Phew, you know how to wear these, you can breathe a bit easier, you ignore the frayed bits and the rips because it all feels comfortable again.

And so it is with patterns of behaviour, folks. The old ones are 'comfortable' because we know how to deal with them, we know what to expect even if that outcome is not what we want consciously. The new behaviours feel brilliant to start with, but then it gets a bit hard to keep it up and after a while it is so easy to slip back into the old, usual ones.

I love this analogy. I use it all the time. Remember those jeans today, put the new pair on, see if you can catch yourself slipping into the old pair and gently bring yourself back to the new pair.

If you keep putting that new pair back on, eventually they will become *just* as comfortable, if not more so, than the old pair and the old pair can go in the bin....

My notes about this page: ○ Read it   ○ Liked it

113

Hey clubbers, how are you?

Today I would like you all to take the advice
of my **incredibly wise** seven-year-old daughter

There's always time to squeeze a little fun in.

My family was on its way out somewhere last weekend and as usual we were running late (I think you're all getting the idea that we are quite often a little tardy). Whilst the grown ups focused on the fact that we were late, my eldest daughter reassured us that everything would be okay because, "there's always time to squeeze a little bit more fun in". What a brilliant mantra for life, what could be more important than squeezing a bit more fun in?

Find the fun today, let go of those grown up hang-ups about time and jobs that need doing and *squeeze* that fun in!

My notes about this page: ○ Read it   ○ Liked it

....

....

....

....

Hello folks!

I caught up with an **old friend** recently

It was lovely to see her, but...

She spent a good amount of our time together telling me about all the things her husband doesn't do. He doesn't clean up after himself very often, he doesn't do the washing, he doesn't do the ironing, he doesn't hoover, he doesn't do the dishwasher as much as she would like him to, he doesn't tidy things away in the way she does, he doesn't buy her flowers, he doesn't like doing some of the things she enjoys, etc. It was quite a long list of things he doesn't do, and they all irritated her.

After a while I asked her what he *does* do. She was stumped. She had a think for a few minutes and then said, "Well, he does play with the children, he does do the cooking a lot, he does do the bins more than me, and he does look after the finances... actually there's quite a lot he does do."

I suggested to her that she started to focus her attention on the things he does do. We all have our own particular strengths and interests, we all have things we are more drawn to doing. Expecting someone else to do the things *you* want them to and then judging them for not doing them, is a tad unfair.

Today, make an effort to appreciate the things that the people around you *do* do instead of getting irritated by the things they don't. It just feels better.

My notes about this page: ○ Read it   ○ Liked it

Hello lovely people, how are you?

I saw a presentation recently that talked about **failure vs. success**

At one point the lady giving the presentation was talking about when she was training as a Life Coach.

She had to do a test over the phone with three top coaches in America.

She was determined to succeed at the test and put her all into preparing for it. Her trainer advised her that failure is not always a bad option as it was often a way of getting some good feedback.

But this lady was set on success, so much so that she passed with flying colours and received absolutely no feedback whatsoever.

One of her fellow trainees however failed the test and was delighted to receive a wealth of feedback, tips and techniques from the three coaches at the top of their game.

So many of us let failure knock us down – believe me if I had allowed that to happen, then my company would have shut its doors about nine months in. I'll tell you that story one day!

Failures are our opportunities to learn, they give us the chance to refine and re-think what we are doing and how we are doing it. The more we can *learn*, the more successful and happy we can be.

My notes about this page: O Read it   O Liked it

_____

_____

_____

_____

Hi there.

Yesterday I talked about **failure** being a wonderful opportunity for feedback and learning

Today is on a similar theme.

As you know, I do a lot of networking in my job and I was at a meeting last week which I really enjoyed. At the end of the meeting one of the guests came up to me and pressed her business card into my hand as she said, "Hi Jo, we met a while ago on a course in Chester, we sat next to each other."

Now I have to be completely honest and say that I didn't recognise her at all. I couldn't remember the last time I'd been on a course in Chester and I had no idea what she was talking about.

But she persisted, "It was a long time ago on a course run by a lady who did business coaching and we all had to stand up at the front and say something, I remember you very well, you had a good impact on me that day, thank you."

I still had no idea what she was talking about and had to admit that I was clueless.

She was not fazed. "I think my speech was a bit rubbish so actually I'm glad that you can't remember it!"

We agreed that we would meet for coffee soon so that she could try and jog my memory further.

I took two things from this very brief encounter which I thought I would share for you to ponder today.

The first is to remember that we very often make a positive impact on other people without even being aware of it. I am so glad that she came and talked to me and made me aware that I had helped her in some way. That feedback gave me a lovely feeling.

The second is that we very often beat ourselves up when we feel that we have done badly at something (as this lady felt with her speech on that course), we believe that everyone around us will have noticed our mistakes, our nerves, etc. The reality is that by and large the only person who notices all those things is ourselves.

Feedback is wonderful stuff folks, make sure you give it *and* ask for it.

My notes about this page: O Read it   O Liked it

....

....

....

....

Hey folks.

Cast your mind back to the last time
you had a **disagreement** with somebody

Could be your partner, your ex, a friend, a colleague.

Whoever it was, how strong was
your urge to get them to see your
point of view and to agree with it?

I have a simple question for you
today, one that very often provokes
discussion and debate.

Do you want to be right or do
you want to be happy?

For me, the answer is very simply the
latter, but we do very much spend
our time striving to be the former.
And no, you can't answer "both"!

When you boil anything right down
to its core, which would *you* choose?

My notes about this page: O Read it   O Liked it

....

....

....

....

Bonjour!

My family and I went on **holiday**
to France last year

One day we ventured out from our holiday camp to get some supplies.

One key thing struck us: we were in France.

Sounds kind of obvious, huh? But when you are staying in a place where most of the guests are British and all of the staff speaks English, it can be easy to forget that you are in a different country.

Now, my French is okay, I lived there for a while about a million years ago so I can understand most stuff and can get by with speaking the basics. However, we found ourselves in a couple of situations on our expedition where language was definitely a barrier. There were some badly constructed French sentences, some sign language and the odd bit of Franglais spoken. But eventually we got there.

And it made me think, there is always a way to communicate. We often get frustrated because we feel that people around us don't understand what we're trying to say. Or that they don't understand how we feel.

Next time you feel like that, I want you to remember me in France, using whatever tools I could to make myself understood, and do the same. I was the one who needed to communicate, the onus was on me, and the responsibility was mine. If you need someone to understand you, there is *always* a way to get your message across.

My notes about this page: ○ Read it   ○ Liked it

Salut! Hope all is well with you.

We had **rather a long journey** to get to our holiday in France, which involved a lot of driving

---

I drove. Partly because we took my car, and partly because I like driving.

During the drive to Folkestone, the girls requested various forms of entertainment. One was to have music playing through an iPod, another was to watch DVDs.

All very clever. And it all required various bits of fiddling by my husband to get the right thing connected to the right bit.

Now, even as little as a year ago, I would have found all the faffing about very distracting. I would have felt the urge, the need, to know exactly what my husband was doing, how and why.

On this journey, I caught myself as the urge appeared. I recognised it

and I reasoned that my attention was needed elsewhere. Driving safely was far more important than knowing what my husband was up to or making sure he pressed the right button. And so I let that urge go, I allowed myself to trust that my husband knew what he was doing and I focused my full attention on my job.

Today I would like to invite you to do the same. Let go of that need to control everything around you, trust that other people know what to do and allow yourself to fully focus just on your part.

Experience how *liberating* that is.

My notes about this page: ○ Read it   ○ Liked it

How are you?

Do you expect everyone around you to be **perfect**?

Do you expect them all to behave in exactly the right way all the time?

Do you think that the people in your life can always say the right thing or do exactly what is needed when it's needed?

I'm betting the answer to those questions is largely "no". That would be unrealistic to expect all that of people, wouldn't it?

So now, ask those same questions about yourself.

I'm betting your answers are somewhat different? We tend to expect much more of ourselves than we do of the people around us.

So, today, ask yourself this question instead, "do I need to be perfect?"

(The answer is *no!*)

My notes about this page: O Read it   O Liked it

Bonjour, clubbers!

We went to **Paris** while we were on our summer holiday last year

---

It was a beautiful sunny day and by mid-afternoon the heat had set in.

We decided to take the Batobus, the boat bus on the River Seine, for a few stops to get us from the Eiffel Tower to Notre Dame.

Every time the boat stopped to pick up more people, we would be sitting in the full heat of the sun, even when we moved to sit in the shade. The heat would get to the point of being almost insufferable and then the boat would move on, the breeze would kick in and relief would come.

I was very aware of this cycle as I sat drifting along and every time the heat got too much I said to myself, "it's ok, this will pass in a minute and that lovely cool breeze will come again".

And so it is with life folks. The heat doesn't last forever, the relief of that breeze will come.

Hold on to that today.

My notes about this page: O Read it   O Liked it

....

....

....

....

Hello there! I hope you're well today.

We spent a lot of our time on holiday
in the **swimming pool**

One day my eldest daughter and I were swimming together.

I challenged her to a race from one side of the pool to the other.

Ready, steady, go! We set off.....
now obviously I was going to let my daughter win but she made it fairly hard because she kept stopping to look over her shoulder and find out where I was.

She was so busy looking behind her, worrying about what I was doing and checking on my progress that she wasn't moving forward herself much at all.

After the third time of checking I said to her, "sweetheart stop looking behind you, look straight ahead and concentrate on going forwards".

'Nuff said huh? Stop looking behind you. Stop focusing on the past, stop being preoccupied with what the others behind you are doing. All that will do is hinder your own progress.

Look straight ahead and focus all your energy on your *journey forwards.*

My notes about this page: O Read it   O Liked it

Hi!

On our last day in France last summer,
we went out for a **family dinner**

The restaurant was a good 10-minute walk from our base.

On the way my youngest daughter said to me, "Mummy, I've got the stitches!"

Now, the advice I was always given about stitch is to keep going, to keep walking until it works its way through and is gone. The instinctive reaction is to stop, but if you do stop it only disappears momentarily and soon returns when you start walking again.

As I explained this to my youngest daughter, it struck me that our emotions work in a very similar way.

If we experience a negative emotion, our instinct is to stop it in its tracks, to halt the effects as soon as possible. But when we do this, the result is only momentary; that negative energy might disappear for a day, a week, a month or a year but it will always come back.

However, if we turn towards it and keep going, work our way through that emotion then, like stitch, it can be more painful for a brief time but we come out the other side and it is gone.

Today have a go at turning towards any negative emotions with acceptance, face them, feel the full force until it subsides and then feel the *relief* of that release.

My notes about this page: ○ Read it   ○ Liked it

Hey there, how are you?

So, yesterday I was **very tired**

I had a long, busy day the day before,
went to bed tired and woke up feeling the same way.

I spent most of the day feeling that way. I'm not good when I'm tired, it makes me grumpy and I find it hard to shake it off. To be honest I spent the day feeling like I'd taken a bit of a backwards step in my usually happy and positive lifestyle.

As I lay in bed on Wednesday night and reflected back over my day, I realised that sometimes a "backward step" is a good thing to experience.

I firmly believe that awareness is the key to life. A handful of years ago I would not have possessed the awareness to recognise a backward step. The very fact that I felt like I had gone backwards showed that I hadn't at all, if that makes sense.

To be able to recognise that then enabled me to re-focus my energy on how I want to be, how I want to act and how I want my life to be. And I reaffirmed my belief that I can choose all of those things.

Once you begin this journey there's no such thing as a backward step, only a *confirmation* of how to go forward.

My notes about this page: O Read it   O Liked it

Hello all!

Something **practical** for you to have a go at today

Get yourself a piece of paper and a pen.

Think of something good, positive and happy that happened to you in the last 24 hours.

Now take just a few minutes and write down everything you can remember about that experience, as many details as you can.

Doing this simple exercise, remembering in this way, marks the experience in your brain as meaningful and embeds it more deeply.

Enjoy!

My notes about this page: ○ Read it   ○ Liked it

....

....

....

....

Happy day, everyone!

The day we arrived back home after our holiday,
we were as **excited** as we had been to go away

...if not more so!

It's such a wonderful feeling to come back to a place that you love, to be back in your own environment, to be surrounded by things that have meaning for you, isn't it?

We all experienced a deep sense of appreciation for our home yesterday. The time away served to remind us how great our normal everyday life is.

Today I want you to look at your home and the things in it in this light; imagine you've been away and just returned home. Nurture that feeling of appreciation for everything in your immediate environment.

Happiness is *coming home*.

My notes about this page: O Read it   O Liked it

Hello one and all!

I want to ask you a **question** today

How do you respond when someone gives you a compliment?

If someone compliments your outfit, do you tell them how cheap it was or how old it is?

If someone compliments your appearance, do you tell them you didn't spend much time getting ready?

If someone compliments your work, do you tell them it was nothing?

If someone compliments your house, do you explain that you haven't had time to clean up and apologise for the mess?

Is your instinctive reaction to shy away from the compliment? To bat it off?

I've asked you all before to take the time and make the effort to give compliments. It boosts the wellbeing of both the giver and the receiver.

However, if you respond to a compliment with a negative comment or an apology or a brick wall, if you throw that compliment back at someone then the opportunity for wellbeing is lost. You are rejecting the compliment and in effect, the giver of that compliment.

Next time someone pays you a compliment, however small, accept it with a smile and a "thank you". Accept it and allow yourself to *feel* it inside.

My notes about this page: ○ Read it   ○ Liked it

Hello there, how are you?

I'm thinking about **weather forecasts** this morning

The band I sing with has an open-air gig soon on a bandstand in a local park.

If it's a sunny day we will obviously have quite a good turnout, if it's cloudy or rainy then we'll probably have trouble getting the band to turn up let alone anyone else!

So I've checked the weather forecast and to be honest it's not looking great. The thing is, if I tell everyone that the weather looks like it's going to be rubbish, then people won't turn up. We all tend to believe what the weather forecast tells us and make our plans accordingly. The forecast is planting an expectation in our minds.

Now actually, anything could happen between now and the gig, it could all change quite easily. And we all know that quite often the weather forecast is wrong. But that expectation has still been planted.

So I'm not telling anyone what the forecast says, in fact I'm going to plant the opposite expectation and see what happens.

Have a go at applying this thought today – is there something that you have a negative expectation about? Is there something that you "know" won't go your way? Flip your mind over to the opposite expectation and see what happens.

Enjoy!

My notes about this page: O Read it   O Liked it

....

....

....

....

Good day!

Today I want you to think about the way that you **say** things

---

How do you express yourself?

My family was enjoying a family meal last Saturday and as we neared the end I said to the girls, "Hands up who wants to come and help Mummy unpack our holiday stuff and tidy up?" My tone of voice was flat, I wasn't expecting them to come and help me, so I put no enthusiasm into my expression. They both shook their heads. I didn't blame them. I wasn't particularly looking forward to doing it myself.

My husband then pointed out that I hadn't made the prospect sound very exciting or appealing, it didn't sound like an enjoyable job.

So I tried again, I jollied my tone up, I made it sound like an adventure was about to be had, I put some enthusiasm into the words. My eldest daughter gave me the same response but my youngest daughter was genuinely more interested in helping me now. Simply by changing the way that I had said the exact same sentence, I had convinced one little girl to join in.

And do you know the best bit? My attitude to the job changed too, I found that I was actually feeling good at the prospect of tackling the suitcases.

So today, before you say something, think about how you are going to say it, put some expression in there, give it some life and see what effect that has – on the people around you, but also on *yourself*.

My notes about this page: ○ Read it   ○ Liked it

_____

_____

_____

_____

Hellooooo! How are you today?

Today I want you to **let the sun shine in yourself**

It will do you good.

Take a couple of minutes. Close your eyes. Picture yourself in a beautiful garden or on a gorgeous beach or in a pretty park. It's a warm, still, sunny day. The sky is beautifully blue, maybe a wisp of white cloud here and there. Imagine yourself sitting in this setting and now feel the rays of the sun shining down on you. Feel yourself absorbing them. Immerse yourself in that lovely warm, comforting feeling.

Then open your eyes. Repeat as often as you like during the day.

Enjoy!

My notes about this page: ○ Read it   ○ Liked it

Hey there my lovelies, how are you?

Today I want you to give yourself permission
at some point to do **absolutely nothing**

Not one single thing.

Take 15 minutes (or longer if you are able) and simply do nowt.

I've invited you to do this before in this book and I shall doubtless invite you to do it again in the future. Why? Because it's important. Believe it or not doing nothing helps to boost productivity, creativity and wellbeing. It gives us the space to pay attention to our feelings and thoughts.

Your brain depends on downtime to recharge and also to process the enormous amount of data we accumulate in our day.

We spend our lives rushing around here, there and everywhere. We feel guilty when we stop and sit down. We get that, "I should be doing something" feeling or as soon as we stop, we see another five thousand things that 'need' our attention.

Notice and accept those thoughts and feelings in yourself when you take that time today but persist in doing nothing.

Give yourself *permission*.

My notes about this page: O Read it   O Liked it

Hello, hello, hello!

Isn't it **amazing** to be alive?

Start your day today with a deep sense of appreciation for simply being alive.

We are brilliant and wonderful beings, the very fact that we have woken up this morning is nothing short of a miracle!

Today I am happy to be alive.

I am going to expand that gratitude out to every living thing that I encounter.

I invite *you* to do the same.

My notes about this page: ○ Read it   ○ Liked it

Hey up clubbers!

I went to see **a client** the other evening

Normally I travel there via dual carriageways and a motorway.

But on the way home this time, my sat nav directed me along the country road route. It made quite a nice change driving along in the countryside as it was going slowly dark around me.

As I drove along I noticed a number of isolated houses, nothing around them but darkness and space. Nobody encroaching on their space and nobody close by to call on if needed. Each one stood completely alone. I know it sounds odd, but I couldn't help but feel a bit sorry for them, they looked lonely.

These houses made me think of us human beings and how sometimes we do the same thing. Sometimes we feel like we want our own space or we don't want to ask for help or we don't feel we deserve other people and we isolate ourselves. We are like those houses, standing alone on a hill, darkness creeping in, nobody to call on if needed.

Human beings are social animals. We need that interaction and stimulus to get us going, to challenge us, to comfort us, to motivate us, to move us forward. Surround yourself with people that you care about and who care about you. And today be *grateful* for those people.

My notes about this page: ○ Read it   ○ Liked it

Hello one and all.

Slow down

That's it, short and simple.

Today make a conscious effort to slow down everything you do and every movement you make, whether you are walking, talking, typing, cooking, writing, breathing, reading, driving, gesturing.

Whatever you do today, have a go at doing it at a slower pace than usual and notice the feeling of calm that naturally appears. Good huh?

Slow yourself down.

My notes about this page: ○ Read it   ○ Liked it

Hello! Is all well in your world?

The girls and I have spent a fair amount
of time **stuck** in traffic jams this summer

What a waste of time, huh?

One day last week, for instance, it took us two and a half hours to get home from a local shopping centre – normally a forty minute journey.

Years ago traffic jams drove me potty and I experienced a lot of them driving up and down the country regularly. I would sit and fume quietly, feeling the pressure mount up, getting angrier and angrier at this obstacle in my life.

And then one day the realisation that there was nothing I could do about being stuck washed over me.

I couldn't control it in any way, shape or form so what was the point in getting myself so wound up? It was a liberating moment and being stuck in traffic has rarely bothered me since.

Today, recognise when you come up against something that you can't control, realise that allowing yourself to become wound up by it is utterly self-destructive and simply *let it go*.

My notes about this page: O Read it   O Liked it

Hello there, how are you?

How often do you **compare yourself to others**?

How often do you think "they do that better than me"?

How often do you think, "they've got more stuff than me"?

How often do you think, "they're a nicer person than me" or " their house is better than mine" or "their car is better than mine" or simply "they are better than me"?

Sound familiar?

How does it make you feel when you compare yourself to others like that?

Not great, huh?

There is a saying that goes, "Don't compare your inside to someone else's outside". Very often we only see the best bits of someone else's life. We don't really know what is actually happening for them or how they are actually feeling. Comparing yourself, warts and all, to someone else's "outside" is a self-destructive act.

Today, have a go at catching yourself when you do it, remind yourself that you don't know their full story, reassure yourself that you are ace (and I know you are all ace) and move on with *your* day.

My notes about this page: O Read it   O Liked it

Greetings all, how are you today?

Do you know, as I sat down to write this
I **couldn't decide** what to write about

I have a list of possible topics to choose from and I couldn't decide which one to cover.

And that in itself told me which one to pick!

How easy do you find it to make decisions?

Do you shy away from it in case your choice is wrong?

Do you hesitate in case the person or people you are with might want something different?

Are you able to make decisions at work but not in your personal life? Or vice versa?

Do you agree with other people's choices, even if it's not what

you would really like, just to make life easier?

Pay attention through the day every time you come up against a decision. Close your eyes briefly and listen to yourself, often you *know* what you want to do so go with your instinct.

If you are genuinely torn between two or more options, then just take a couple of minutes and imagine the scenario of each option. Go with the one that feels good and right, you will know which one that is.

Trust yourself.

My notes about this page:　　　　　　　　　○ Read it　　○ Liked it

....

....

....

....

Welcome to today, woohoo!

It was my turn to **put the girls to bed** last night

Which means lots of lovely cuddles, hoorah!

Our eldest daughter is something of a chatterbox. Bless her. After about 20 minutes of non-stop chatter, I asked her to go to sleep. She said okay and we both closed our eyes. A couple of minutes later, I opened my eyes and looked at her. She was lying there with her eyes closed but completely squeezed up, forcing them to be shut really tightly.

I smiled as she said to me, "Mummy I can't get to sleep, no matter how hard I try", and then I explained that she was trying too hard. Squeezing her eyes up like that was tensing them instead of relaxing them, which is what you need to do to go to sleep.

In the effort of trying so hard, she was doing the exact opposite of what she actually needed to do.

Is there something you want to achieve for yourself?

Is there something that is eluding you no matter how hard you try?

Are you trying too hard?

Let go of those reins just a little bit, don't hold on so hard, relax your eyes a bit and *see* what happens.

My notes about this page: O Read it   O Liked it

....

....

....

....

Happy day everyone!

Hands up if you have a **lucky charm** of some sort?

A lucky piece of clothing or jewellery, a lucky something on your key ring or a lucky ornament?

I like wearing rings with big stones. It's a fairly rare day when one isn't adorning my right hand. When I started wearing them a long time ago, I was very much using them as a sort of lucky charm, a confidence booster if you will. This lovely, glamorous ring on my finger somehow allowed my personality to be bigger and me to feel more confident.

I would choose which ring I was going to wear very carefully each day; if something good had happened last time I wore one, then it would get picked regularly because it was "lucky".

Now obviously, rings don't actually have magical powers (don't tell my girls that till they are a bit older though please). I knew that all along and gradually I realised that good things came because, by using the rings, I was opening myself up to those things and allowing them in. I acknowledged that the ring was a comfort, but the power was me.

So if you have a lucky charm of some sort, make good use of it, if it helps you, use it often, but realise that it is simply a stepping stone.

You are your own lucky charm.

My notes about this page: ○ Read it ○ Liked it

Hey clubbers!

Right, I'm looking at **powerful body language** today

I have a simple technique for you to try that will give you confidence and a feeling of power in any situation.

Cool, huh?

Who has heard of Wonder Woman? I may have wanted to be Wonder Woman quite badly when I was a little girl! Can you remember her stance? Feet a bit wider than hip width apart, standing up tall and straight with her hands on her hips?

Set a timer on your phone or tablet or computer for two minutes. Then stand like Wonder Woman for those two minutes. Alternatively, you can stand with your feet a bit wider than hip width apart and your arms up in the air above your head.

Believe it or not, standing in one of these "power poses" for just two minutes significantly increases the level of testosterone and decreases the level of cortisol in your system. High levels of testosterone increase your feeling of pride and boost your self image. Cortisol is the stress hormone so any decrease there is ace.

So today, have a go at being Wonder Woman, just for two minutes, any time that you feel like you need a power surge.

Enjoy!

My notes about this page: ○ Read it   ○ Liked it

Hey up, folks.

Is there a **difficult person** in your life?

Someone who you dread seeing, even if it's not very often?

Someone that rubs you up the wrong way or irritates you? Someone who just brings out that negative vibe in you? It might be an ex, a family member, a friend, it might even be yourself.

Today I am going to invite you to find one positive thing about that person. Bring them to mind and ponder them until you find just one good thing, anything at all, big or small.

Now focus all your attention on that positive thing. Every time you think about that person, just think about that good thing. Whenever you see them, just see that one positive thing. Then notice how your perception of them and feelings towards them gradually shift.

Start with one positive thing.

Enjoy!

My notes about this page:　　　　　　　　　　　○ Read it　　○ Liked it

Helloooo!

A friend of mine **posted** on Facebook last night

"It's so hard watching someone else living my dream and loving it."

My comment on her post was, "What is your dream and why aren't you living it?"

Folks, you do know that there is no earthly reason why you can't live your dream, don't you? You do know that you absolutely have the power to achieve anything that you want? You do know that the only thing that stands in the way of anything is yourself?

I feel so passionately about this; we limit ourselves all the time, hold ourselves back from things we want because we're "not good enough" or "it's not realistic" or we "don't deserve it" or "that's not the kind of thing that happens to me" or "that only happens for other people".

Nope, I'm not having it folks, put your self-belief hat on right now and go out there and get what you want.

Don't watch other people doing it, live your dream and love it.

That's an *order*.

My notes about this page: ○ Read it   ○ Liked it

Hello again, how are you?

My lovely husband and I were watching an **adventure superhero type programme** on telly last night

---

There were several moments of peril for the hero during the course of the episode.

During the first dangerous encounter I entered into the drama of it, I was concerned for the hero's welfare, jumpy in case the worst happened. I could feel my heart racing as a panicky feeling caught hold in my chest. And then there was the relief when he came out as the victor, hoorah.

The second time he was in a bad situation I felt those same feelings begin to build. Then a thought came into my head, "He's the hero of this entire programme, they are not going to kill him off, he's going to be absolutely fine."

Instantly relief flooded my system, the panic and drama melted away, I could watch the proceedings calmly and fully enjoy them.

Today I want you to realise that you are that hero. You are going to be absolutely fine. Whatever you are going through, at this moment or in the future, you will come out the other side as the victor.

Keep that thought in your mind, let the drama unfold without immersing yourself too fully in it and *feel* the relief of knowing that all is well.

My notes about this page: O Read it   O Liked it

Hello there.

Okey dokey, a few pages ago I asked you
to think of a **difficult person** in your life

I asked you to find one positive thing about them, then to focus on that good thing whenever you met.

Today I want you to apply this
technique to yourself but expand
it slightly.

Get a piece of paper and on it write
three good things about you, your
personality or characteristics. Not
three good things generally in your
life, not three good things that are
around you, not three good things
that are external – all of those belong
to a different technique.

Nope, I want you to identify three
good things that are within you.

Here's mine: I am caring, I am fun,
I like cuddling.

Once you have written down
your three positive things, take a
couple of moments to focus your
attention on those qualities and feel
appreciation for them.

Then continue to pay attention to
those qualities all day today and
beyond, please. If it helps, fold
that piece of paper up and put it
somewhere accessible – your purse/
wallet, the pocket of whatever you're
wearing today. Then you can check
it any time you feel a bit bleurgh or
simply want to focus your attention
on what it is that makes you so ace.

Enjoy!

My notes about this page: O Read it   O Liked it

Hi all and how are you today?

The girls and I went out with some friends
to a **small animal petting farm** yesterday

While we were there, my youngest daughter fell over and grazed her right elbow.

There was some blood, quite a few tears, a lot of cuddles. It hurt, that much was obvious.

It took a few minutes to calm her down and then we washed the graze and I gave it a magic kiss to make it better. Within ten minutes of the 'incident' my youngest daughter was back having fun with her friends, feeding the animals, running around and laughing again.

I've suggested before that we study children for our life lessons. I think they can teach us a lot. Once my youngest daughter had let her hurt and sadness come up, released her feelings about what happened, been reassured that she was okay and that the cut would heal, she moved on.

She accepted that the cut was there. That it would hurt for a bit but that fundamentally she was okay.

No wallowing, no soul searching, no harking back to past incidents that were similar, no fretting that something similar might happen at a future point. She simply moved on.

She moved on because what was most important to her was to have fun and enjoy herself. To feel good.

Take a leaf out of my daughter's book today. If you are hurt, acknowledge it, let those feelings come up. Reassure yourself or ask someone to reassure you that you are okay, you will heal.

It might hurt for a bit but not forever, accept that. Don't allow that hurt to pull you back into the past or affect your thoughts about the future.

Move on and focus on doing something to make yourself feel good, there is *nothing* more important in life.

My notes about this page: O Read it   O Liked it

Hey up folks.

I'm continuing the story of my daughter's **accident** at the farm today

---

It happened when we were feeding the baby goats (who were very cute incidentally).

We had bought bags of food and the kids were grabbing handfuls of food, running to the fence, giving it to a goat and then running back to grab another handful.

At the time of the 'incident', I was kneeling by the fence with a couple of the children feeding a baby goat. My daughter came over, grabbed some food, turned around and tripped straight over the legs of her friend who was sitting beside me. As I mentioned yesterday, blood and tears and cuddles ensued.

Once my daughter had calmed down she turned to her friend and said, "Say sorry! You tripped me up." Her friend was most adamant that she hadn't tripped my daughter up at all. On our walk to the sinks to get my daughter's cut cleaned up she was hell bent on blaming her friend for the fact that she was hurt. After a few minutes of listening to my daughter blame her, her friend started to get defensive and shout back. This was the point at which I stepped in.

I stepped in and explained to my daughter that she had tripped over her friend's legs because she wasn't looking where she was going, because she wasn't paying attention properly. I explained that to blame someone or something else for your own mistake was not the right thing to do and indeed would only cause arguments between two people who had previously liked each other. By the time we reached the sinks, my daughter had apologised to her friend and they were friends again.

We are each responsible for ourselves and our own actions. If you get hurt, don't look around for the nearest person to blame, even if that person is yourself. Blame causes upset, hurt, fights and broken relationships.

Catch yourself today.

Notice your reaction when something negative happens.

Are you *looking* for someone to blame?

My notes about this page: O Read it   O Liked it

Hellooooooo!

It's the last installment of my daughter's **grazed arm story** this morning, are you sitting comfortably?

Then I'll begin....

That evening, once we were back home safely and the girls were tucked up in bed, I was giving my youngest daughter her goodnight cuddles and she said "Ooh, Mummy my cut elbow hurts when I stretch my arm out." And she demonstrated by stretching her arm out and wincing. Bless her. My response was to say, "Well, don't stretch your arm out then."

And I got an immediate flashback to being a girl myself. One of the things I always remember about my dad was that if I said to him, "doing this hurts" or "when I do this I don't like it" his response would always be, "well, don't do that then."

Do you know, it used to really annoy me when he said it to me. I can remember thinking to myself, "Well that's a silly answer, as if I can just stop doing that."

And that night with my daughter, I realised how wise my lovely dad had actually been. We spend our lives repeating patterns over and over, patterns that we know deep down aren't good for us, and patterns that we know deep down will hurt us. And yet we persist.

The truth is, if you know that doing something is going to hurt then you can absolutely stop yourself from doing it. Breaking those patterns is utterly within your control.

Don't *purposely* put yourself in harm's way, if it hurts when you stretch your arm out, then don't stretch your arm out.

My notes about this page: ○ Read it   ○ Liked it

Hello there, folks!

I want to talk about **eye contact** today

People who make and maintain eye contact are perceived as reliable, honest, sociable and confident.

So it follows that if someone's gaze refuses to meet your eyes, then it sends feelings of dishonesty, insecurity, dislike or shyness.

Eye contact is a sign that you are a good listener. It shows that you are paying attention to the other person and they will be more likely to trust and respect you.

Non-verbal communication is a vital part of communication as a whole, and maintaining good eye contact in particular, is a brilliant way of building connections with other people and connections with other people are a massive part of happiness.

So today, practice making and keeping eye contact. Start by practicing with yourself in the mirror – after all if you can't look yourself in the eye then it will be difficult to meet other people's eyes.

Spend just a few minutes this morning looking yourself in the eye, pay attention to any feelings that brings up for you. And then be conscious today of making good eye contact with those around you – see how it opens up those conversations, connections and relationships.

My notes about this page: O Read it   O Liked it

Hello all, how are we today?

It's a **simple one** today, folks

Try this out...

Every time you feel negative, or come up against something negative today, I want you to very simply close your eyes, take a deep breath in and as you exhale say, "all is well". Allow yourself to feel the power of those words, say them with feeling and conviction, and say them out loud if you can.

Because all is well, *I promise*, all is well.

My notes about this page: ○ Read it   ○ Liked it

....

....

....

....

Hey up clubbers, how's it going?

Do you know that **no** thought is true?

The average person has between *50 and 70 thousand* thoughts a day.

A day! And not one of them is true, not one. They are just something that you think, that's all.

A thought is simply something that you, at a particular moment in time, give your attention to. It is that attention that makes the thought appear real.

The more attention that you give to the thought, the more you think it. And the more you think it, the more attention you give to it. And the more attention you give to it, the more you think it. And so on and so on until the thought becomes so strong that it becomes a belief.

And now you believe it, now it has a bit of power. But guess what? If no thought is true, then no belief is true either.

If it is your attention that gives your thoughts their power, then all you have to do is take the attention away. And hey presto, the power is gone.

So give that attention to the thoughts that deserve it, and disempower the rest.

Can you see how the power is in *your* hands?

My notes about this page:

○ Read it   ○ Liked it

Hello folks.

How do you feel **right now**?

Take a moment and ask yourself that simple question.

I believe awareness is the key to forging a good, happy life. If you are unaware of something, then it is a tad hard to do anything about it. Largely, we plod through life completely unaware of the myriad of feelings and emotions that flood our bodies and minds every day.

So, how do you feel right now? Check in with yourself and find out, give your feelings some attention in this moment.

Your challenge today is to make a conscious effort to ask yourself that same question a number of times throughout the day.

If you think you might forget to do it, then take your phone or tablet or whatever device you use and set yourself 10 reminder alerts at random times. Every time one goes off, ask yourself, "how do I feel right now?"

Start *building* that awareness.

My notes about this page: ○ Read it   ○ Liked it

Helloooo everyone!

Hands up if you have **an inner voice**

You know, the one...

It tells you you've done something wrong or that you're rubbish or that you shouldn't wear that or look like this or behave like that or reach for that goal?

Does that sound familiar?

Believe it or not, that voice is on your side. It is part of your subconscious mind and its job is to protect you. It genuinely believes that by stopping you from doing something, or trying something, or wearing something, or having something, it is protecting you from some kind of harm.

So today I want you to engage that voice in conversation.

Next time you hear it tell you that you can't possibly do, or have, or try something, just pause and give it your attention. Don't try and bat it away or ignore it as we do with so many negative things.

Ask it where that opinion is really coming from and what it is trying to achieve.

Listen to the answers that come up and make peace with them.

You will find after time that *they* make peace with you too.

My notes about this page: ○ Read it   ○ Liked it

Hello, how are you?

Yesterday was a lovely **mooching-about** day at our house

We played games and got some little jobs done.

In the late afternoon, I took the girls out on their bikes around the local roads. They both love cycling, and since my youngest daughter learnt to ride without stabilizers, there's no stopping them.

The pavements around us are generally wide and perfect for little girls on bikes to practice their skills. Both of my girls are confident at cycling and love going as fast as they can. After a while I noticed something interesting.

When the pavement was completely clear, they both cycled fast and completely straight. No wobbles, no doubts, no nerves.

However, as soon as there was a potential obstacle in sight – a parked car, a bin, a tree – both of them immediately slowed down and began to wobble all over the place.

In every case, if they had simply kept cycling straight and true, as they did when the pavement was clear, they would have breezed past every obstacle. But in their efforts to avoid the obstacle, they actually increased their chances of crashing into it.

And I thought to myself how true that is in life – we allow the obstacles to make us wobble, to make us doubt our own ability.

If we simply kept going, focused on the path ahead, confident of our ability, straight and true, then we would breeze past every little obstacle that appeared.

Keep this analogy in mind as you go through today. Picture yourself on your bike breezing past those obstacles.

Stay *straight* and *true*.

My notes about this page: O Read it   O Liked it

Hey clubbers!

The Big Band I sing with had a **wedding gig** at the weekend

It was about an hour's drive away from me, so I used that time to rehearse my songs.

The Bride and Groom had requested, "Nobody Does It Better" as the song for their First Dance. This was the very first song I ever sang with the band, in fact it was the song I was asked to sing at my audition 12 years ago.

Driving along singing that song, took me back 12 years. I remembered how nervous I had been at the audition. I remembered how nervous I had been at the first gig. I remembered how nervous I had been at a lot of the subsequent gigs. I remembered that the whole thing had scared the pants off me as well as being something that I desperately wanted to do.

I also recognised how much my confidence has grown over the years. My voice has improved, my technique has improved, and my inhibitions have all but disappeared. I still get nervous before gigs, but the constant practice has given me confidence in my ability and the knowledge that I *can* do this.

The point is that if I had allowed my fear to swallow me up 12 years ago, I would have missed out on one of the best experiences of my life. I would have missed out on that learning, that practice, that knowledge. I would have missed that opportunity to grow my self-confidence.

So, what is it that you really want to do but are scared to try? What would you love to do but don't feel confident about?

Take one small step towards that thing today, whatever it is. Know that however nervous you might feel now, with time and practice, your confidence can only grow.

Put your foot on *that* path.

My notes about this page: O Read it   O Liked it

Hello there.

A few weeks ago, I was driving through a **rundown** area of Liverpool

---

After a few minutes, I realised that I was mentally ticking off negative things as I drove along.

There was a large pile of rubbish on one side of the road, the person in front of me was driving somewhat erratically, the houses I was driving past looked drab and depressing, there was a funny smell in the air etc.

Now, I love Liverpool, so as soon as I recognised that I was noticing all these negative things, I made a conscious decision to start finding the good things around me. The sun was shining, the erratic driver turned off. There was a house with beautiful hanging baskets outside it, some people walking past had smiles on their faces and so on.

I made a choice as to where I put my attention. It gave me nicer thoughts and a good feeling.

So today I have a challenge for you.

Every time you recognise that you have clocked something negative – externally or internally – I want you to make that same choice. As soon as something negative comes into your mind, I want you to make a conscious effort to find some positive things, the more the better. Your attention will drift off again during the day so don't beat yourself up about it, simply notice when you have a negative thought and bring your attention back round to something positive.

The more you practice it, the more naturally it will come.

Enjoy!

My notes about this page: ○ Read it   ○ Liked it

Hey there, how are you?

I was talking to a **friend** yesterday

She was explaining to me how she had always felt left out of things.

When she was a child, she was largely alone at school, not many friends, was never asked to play or picked for the sports team, she simply didn't fit in. This feeling had carried through into adulthood.

During the course of the conversation, I asked her to close her eyes and imagine herself in the playground. In her picture she was on her own, watching the other kids play around her, unable to join in. I asked her to pick a group of children that she would like to play with and to imagine she was approaching them. Then, I suggested that she ask if she could join in with their game.

She did, and to her great surprise, they said yes! A big smile flashed across her face. As she opened her eyes she said, "It never even occurred to me to ask!"

This lovely lady had spent her life believing that people wouldn't want to play with her, that they wouldn't want her to join in, so she had never actually asked for herself.

Is there something you want for yourself? Do you feel left out of anything? Do you believe others won't allow it?

Have you *asked*?

My notes about this page: ○ Read it   ○ Liked it

Hi all!

Is there someone **disapproving** in your life?

Someone who watches what you do with pursed lips and a frown?

Someone who is vocal about their dislike of your words and actions?

When someone disapproves, it means they are judging you by their own limiting beliefs. Not yours. I promise you that their disapproval says more about them than it does about you.

What does it actually say about you?

Not one single thing.

If it says nothing about you, then very simply let it bounce off you, no need to take it on board, no need to absorb it, let it go.

Simple.

My notes about this page: ○ Read it   ○ Liked it

_____

_____

_____

_____

Hello there! How are you today?

I had a **lovely** day yesterday

A bit of morning networking followed by a one to one session with a client, followed by a new client at home.

Let's call my lovely client Bob, and my new client Frank.

Bob lives about 40 minutes away from me and I left his place a little late. So I sent a message to Frank to let him know I would be about 15 minutes late. "No problem", came the reply.

Then I got stuck in traffic, *lots* of traffic. Time ticked by, so I sent another message to Frank to say I would be another 15 minutes late.

Eventually, it became obvious that I wasn't going to make it back in time for our appointment, so I messaged Frank to suggest we rearrange. Frank was fine with that and we have agreed another date to start the sessions.

Simple, huh?

The point of telling you this story, is that years ago, this very same

situation would have sent me into a spiral of panic, guilt, anxiety and beating myself up for being rubbish. Yesterday, it didn't bother me at all. I remained calm and philosophical about the whole thing.

Because the circumstances were entirely out of my control, there was absolutely nothing I could have done to change the situation. And if it was out of my control, then who am I damaging by reacting with panic or guilt or anxiety or by beating myself up or by all of the above?

Me.

And do you know what? I don't want to damage me.

Next time you find yourself in a situation that is out of your control, take a moment to recognise that fact, nip that panic or guilt or anxiety in the bud, and don't damage you.

My notes about this page: O Read it   O Liked it

Hi everyone!

Yesterday, I told you about **Bob** and **Frank**

Also, I told you about me being late for Frank's appointment due to traffic.

I wanted to expand on that story today by looking at my past reaction of panic, anxiety and guilt.

The reason that I would have experienced those emotions years ago, is because I would have felt like I was letting Frank down. I would have been worried about what Frank thought of me. Would Frank be in a mood with me, or would I get into trouble? Would he think I was silly, inept or useless, and what if the situation made him not want to book another appointment with me? If he decided not to rebook, then what would he tell other people? Would he tell them I was useless? Would he advise people not to book with me either? What would that mean for my business, would my whole business collapse because I annoyed Frank, and if my business collapsed, then what would my family do, where would we live, how would we feed ourselves, how would I look after my gorgeous girls, would the whole world end???????

What are you thinking as you read the above? Is there a small smile on your face at the absurdity of the thought process?

It's fairly obvious that missing one appointment with Frank is not going to result in any of those imagined scenarios. And, 99.999999% of the time, the reality of a situation is nowhere close to the negative possibilities we imagine for ourselves.

When you find yourself in a situation where your brain starts running away with you, I want you to fast forward to the absolute worst result you can think of.

Bring it to mind, and allow that same small smile to creep across your face as you realise how utterly *unlikely* it is to actually happen.

My notes about this page: ○ Read it   ○ Liked it

Hey there.

It's the **last instalment** of the Bob & Frank story today

Are you ready?

I read back over yesterday's post and this bit stood out for me:

"I would have been worried about what Frank thought of me, whether Frank would be in a mood with me...would he think I was silly, inept or useless?"

We expend a lot of energy and headspace worrying and fretting over what other people think of us. We imagine that people are saying all kinds of negative things about us and we wonder what we can do about it.

The fact is, you have no control over what someone else thinks of you. I will probably never find out exactly what Frank was thinking when he got my messages to say I would be late, then later, then not coming at all. He may very well have thought I was inept or useless. He may very well have been disgruntled and annoyed.

But Frank's feelings and thoughts come from Frank's beliefs about the world and how it 'should' work. I have absolutely no control over those, nor can I change them, only Frank can do that.

The only things I *can* control are my thoughts and feelings. I rationalised the situation for myself, and realised it was out of my control, made peace with that fact and felt fine.

Make peace with yourself. What others think about you is none of your business and need not affect you at all.

Have fun!

My notes about this page: O Read it   O Liked it

Hey up, folks.

I have a **confession** to make

My name is Jo and I have bingo-wings.

Now, before you all start being lovely and telling me that I don't and that I'm nice and slim, let me just assure you that I really do. My upper arms are chunky, a bit flabby and they wobble when I clap or wave.

Bingo-wings.

They have been gradually growing over the last few years and I've been ignoring them. Last week, I found myself acknowledging the fact that they are there, and this thought popped into my head, "ah well, I guess I'm getting to the age where things like this happen, where everything starts to droop a bit."

The minute that thought came into my head, my brain went, "What?! I beg your pardon? Are you simply going to roll over and adopt that attitude?! Who said it's age related? Who says you have to just accept it?!"

I was quite surprised by the vehemence with which my brain reacted, to be honest. It made me realise how often we all do that in life – we simply accept the status quo.

We believe that there isn't really anything we can do to change things. We bumble on saying, "oh well, it's always been like that, it's just the way things are" or "oh, it's because of my age, or my hormones, or my personality."

So I wanted to make this distinction for you all. I heartily believe in accepting myself and where I am in my life right now. I believe that allows me to move forward in the right way. It does not mean that I can't change things, it does not mean that I just lie down and say "ah, well that's just the way it is" when there is the potential for something better.

For now, I accept the fact that I have bingo-wings, and I know the ability to change that is totally within my power. I might not be completely ready to start the process yet, it will take some work, dedication and time, but I know that if I'm willing to do it then I can change anything.

So can you.

My notes about this page: ○ Read it   ○ Liked it

....

....

....

....

Hello one and all.

How "**should**" you feel today?

What "should" you be doing?

When "should" you have achieved everything by?

Where "should" you be?

Why "should" you?

I will have mentioned to some of you in the past that I dislike the word "should". It's a word that we use all the time, in general conversation, about ourselves and others. We talk about all the things we "should" do and all the ways we "should" feel. It has become one of those throwaway words that we use all the time without really thinking about it.

But "should" implies a lack of self-acceptance and puts us under pressure to be a certain way, to conform to a set of beliefs that may not be ours. It is just another tool with which to beat ourselves up:

"I should have done it this way"

"I should be feeling this way"

"I shouldn't have said that".

Today I want you to be conscious of the number of times you use the word "should". Notice each time it comes out of your mouth, recognise that you are judging yourself, pressuring yourself and then ask yourself:

"Why should I?"

My notes about this page: O Read it   O Liked it

....

....

....

....

Hello, hello, hello.

Now, we spend the vast majority of our time **at work**

So it stands to reason that if we want to be happy people, then we need to be happy in our work.

The obvious next question is whether you feel valued in your work, by your boss (if you have one) or your colleagues or your clients? It's a key question when people talk about stress in the workplace. Employers are encouraged to make their employees feel valued and appreciated.

I would like to pose a different question.

Do *you* value what you do?

Because let's face it folks, if you do not appreciate and believe how awesome you are at whatever it is that you do, then how can you be happy doing it?

Grab a piece of paper and a pen. Now, write down at least five things that make you fantastic at your job.

Here is mine:

I care.

I never judge.

I listen.

I am good at presenting.

I have a good voice for it!

Write yours and put that piece of paper somewhere in your work area, on the wall, in a frame on the shelf, on your desk, somewhere in your eye-line.

Value you.

Go!

My notes about this page: ○ Read it   ○ Liked it

Hello there, how are you?

Today is a **simple one** my lovelies

Take a couple of minutes and find something beautiful.

It can be anything – a picture of someone you love, a flower, a painting, a sunrise, a sunset, an animal, an ornament, you choose.

Whatever it is, find something beautiful. Now give it your undivided attention for five minutes. Pay attention to every single detail of that thing, notice all its colours, shapes, lines. Notice it in all its glory, drink that beauty in.

Then go about your business and anytime you feel a bit bleurgh during the day, just go back and give that thing your attention again for a few minutes.

There is so much beauty in the world, give it your attention and allow it to make you feel good.

Enjoy!

My notes about this page: O Read it   O Liked it

....

....

....

....

Helloooo.

Last week I emailed a contact to **follow up** an enquiry about a workshop

---

Yesterday I received their reply.

It showed up as a notification on my phone first. I was in a meeting so couldn't check the whole message immediately but the line that I could see was "Hi Jo, thanks for your email, I'm not....."

My instinctive reaction was that the rest of that email would contain a negative response. I got that slight sinking feeling in my tummy and the, "oh well, better luck next time" thought process.

A couple of hours later, I got the chance to check the email properly and the full sentence read, "Hi Jo, thanks for your email, I'm not in the office at the moment so will come back to you properly next week to set a date for the workshop."

Not a negative response at all, in fact, the exact opposite. It gave me a jolt to realise that my assumption and expectation had been that the response would be negative.

How often do you ask a question expecting a negative response?

Are you waiting for people to reject you or accept you? Which do you believe they will do?

Pay attention today to that gut feeling. Notice if you're expecting the good or the bad. Allow that realisation to come up to the surface and make a conscious effort to flip it around.

The results may very well *amaze* you.

My notes about this page: ○ Read it   ○ Liked it

Hey there all!

So today I want to talk to you about **caffeine**

Hands up if you enjoy a nice cup of coffee?

Hands up if you like to relax with a lovely cup of tea?

We all think that caffeine boosts our energy levels, but actually it is quite simply a chemical stimulant. We may well experience a perceived energy rise as the positive messengers in our brain are boosted, but then we will experience the side effect of fatigue as our energy levels fall.

And when they fall what do we reach for? More caffeine to send us soaring again. If we do this too often, then the negative effects increase: lack of concentration, restlessness, inability to sleep effectively, irritability and an increase in the stress hormones cortisol and adrenaline.

If you are feeling stressed, then your body is in a state of heightened stimulation. So, if you have a cup of tea to 'relax' what you are actually doing is putting a stimulant into an already over-stimulated body.

Have a go at switching to the decaf version of whatever you drink. Your body will thank you for it.

Honestly!

My notes about this page: O Read it   O Liked it

Hello again everyone!

I'm all about **spreading some love** today

We've done similar stuff to this in the past, but you can never have too much love.

So, we're doing it again!

Today, I want you to take every single opportunity you possibly can to tell everyone that you come into contact with that you love them.

If you're texting or messaging someone, then put "I love you" somewhere into the message.

If you're with people, then put those three words into the conversation at some point. If you're arguing with someone, then tell them you love them. If you're cuddling someone, say those words. If you're with a friend and have never told them that you love them, do it now.

You do not need a special reason to tell someone that you love them. You do not need to wait until something special happens. Never assume that people know how you feel. Tell them. Tell them all the time.

It will make them smile. It will make them feel good.

It will make you smile. It will make you feel good.

Enjoy!

My notes about this page: O Read it   O Liked it

Hello there, how are you?

Last night my husband and I settled down
to watch the new episode of **Dr Who**

There was a scene fairly early on that involved a young boy in peril.

He was trapped in a field surrounded by mines with no clear way out. Alone, stuck and somewhat doomed.

Then the Doctor appeared, out of nowhere. He said to the boy, "You have a one in 1000 chance of survival......so let's forget all the other chances and focus on that one..."

Brilliant!

Couldn't have put it better myself.

What do we do when we're in trouble? We focus all our attention on the million and one things that could go wrong, on the thousands of different ways we could fail, on the hundreds of ways it could get worse.

Today I am challenging you to think like the Doctor. Give all your attention to that one chance that everything will work out just the way you want it to. If those other 999 possibilities come in to your head, smile at them and turn your attention back to that one brilliant, fantastic, amazing, possible chance.

Enjoy!

My notes about this page: O Read it   O Liked it

Hi clubbers!

I've been a little **under the weather** for a few days now

I'm coming out the other side of it today, so I'm sure I'll be back on my feet properly tomorrow.

What do you do when you're ill? Do you soldier on regardless? Do you continue working at the same pace, cramming everything in to your schedule, worried about letting other people down, being brave and going into work in case your boss is annoyed, making sure that project you are working on is done by you because nobody else could possibly complete it?

Have you heard of presenteeism? It is the act of going to work whilst sick, sickness presence at work rather than sickness absence. It is also defined as the act of putting in more hours at work than is needed for effective performance.

When you go to work ill, you may tell yourself that you are doing everyone else a favour by turning up. You may tell yourself that you risk getting the sack if you don't turn up. You may tell yourself that you can't afford not to turn up.

Actually, when you go to work ill, what you are likely to do is reduce your productivity, increase the length of time you may be ill for, increase the likelihood of becoming ill again, pass the germs on to your colleagues and make mistakes that you wouldn't ordinarily make.

So I'm off back to bed now, to give myself the proper time to rest and recuperate so that I can be fighting fit tomorrow and able to perform properly. I hope that next time you feel under the weather, you give *yourself* the same treatment.

My notes about this page: O Read it   O Liked it

....

....

....

....

Helloo, how are you?

This day of the week is a **bit special** in my family

My eldest daughter is allowed to stay up a bit later than her younger sister.

This means that my lovely hubby and I get some one to one time with each of the girls. My youngest daughter has decided that what she would like to do during this time is to snuggle up in bed and watch a film on the iPad.

Last night however, she spent so long getting ready for bed that I heard myself saying, "Come on sweetheart, the longer you take to get ready the less time you get to watch the film."

It's a fair enough point, but as soon as the words were out of my mouth, I realised that what I could have said was, "Come on sweetheart, the quicker you get ready the more time you have to watch the film."

Now, effectively I'm saying the same thing in both cases, right? Except the second version is a lot more positive and appealing.

In the first version, she is losing something, in the second she is gaining. I know which version I would respond more favourably to.

I've discussed with some of you in the past that, as human beings, we find it much easier to see the negative side of life. I firmly believe that part of the reason for that is buried in the way we were spoken to as children – simply switching the framing of a sentence from a negative slant to a positive one can have a massive effect.

I didn't catch myself in time last night, but I will in future.

Have a go today at catching those negative sentences before they come out of your mouth. Switch them around to the positive version and see what an improved response you get, from yourself and those around you.

Enjoy!

My notes about this page: ○ Read it ○ Liked it

....

....

....

....

Hey up all, how are you today?

I mentioned that I was in Reading recently
running **a workshop**

I drove down to Bristol on Wednesday evening.

I stayed with my beautiful sister and her family before driving over to Reading on Thursday morning.

On my travels along various motorways, I noticed something. There are a lot of bad drivers around.

People who don't indicate. Who pull in front of you at speed. Who drive right up behind you at speed. People who obviously have somewhere incredibly important to be in five minutes' time. Who either believe that putting everyone's lives in danger is okay or who haven't stopped to think about the possible consequences of their actions.

Within the first hour of my journey down to Bristol, I had had three near misses with people pulling across directly in front of me with no indicating. My impulse each time it happened was to get annoyed, to beep my horn or flash my lights or shout something rude. After talking about emotions yesterday, my awareness of my own emotional state was heightened and so I employed the following technique.

I asked myself, "What don't I want out of this situation?"

The answer was, "to get angry and wound up in myself."

The next question was, "So what *do* I want out of this situation?" And the answer was, "to remain calm and focused on my own driving."

The last question was, "*Why*, why do I want that?" And the answer was very simply, "because it feels better, because I will drive better and that means I will get home to my family safely."

Giving myself the headspace to ask those questions took about 10 seconds, but it completely changed the way I reacted to every subsequent driver.

With that invaluable knowledge, it was then easy for me to calm my system down with a few deep breaths and a smile on my face.

Have a go at using this technique yourself today and any time you find yourself in a negative situation, or feeling negatively about something. Take control of that response.

Enjoy!

My notes about this page: ○ Read it   ○ Liked it

....

....

....

....

Hey folks.

A while ago, I invited you to think of a difficult person in your life and find one good, **positive** thing about them

---

Something that you could focus on when dealing with them rather than seeing all the negatives.

Sometimes it can be really hard to find something positive about the person in question! So I thought we would revisit this in a slightly different way.

If there is someone you have a difficult relationship with at the moment, then I would wager it hasn't always been the case? There must have been a time, however fleeting, when the relationship between you was easier. I would like you to take a few minutes, close your eyes and turn your attention back to that time.

Immerse yourself in remembering how that person was back then, what you liked about them, how you felt about them and how your relationship with each other was. Allow the good feelings to flow through your body as you think about it all, allow that smile to creep on to your face. Do you feel a bit better towards them now? Hold on to that. Repeat as necessary.

Enjoy!

My notes about this page: O Read it   O Liked it

....

....

....

....

Hellooo again, everyone!

When I see individual clients, I quite often send them a **recording** to listen to in between sessions

A new client returned for their second session with me the other day.

When I asked if they had listened to the recording I sent, the answer was, "No". And the no was swiftly followed by the claim "I simply haven't had the time."

The recording is 18 minutes long.

The recording would have enabled the client to relax every day, to have some positive stuff going into their minds every day, to put their foot on the path of happiness every single day.

But they didn't have time for themselves.

Now, don't get me wrong, there is no judgment here. This is entirely the client's choice. I am not here to tell them off. This story simply struck me as indicative of what most people do.

They don't make the time for themselves. They don't take the time out of their day to make sure that they are okay.

There may be a million and one reasons behind this, but the fact remains that just 20 minutes a day could make all the difference between mediocrity and happiness and when I put it like that it's a no-brainer, huh?

Today's thought is to urge you all to put the time in, even if you believe that you're not good enough, or you don't deserve it, or you're too stuck in your ways, or you simply don't have enough space in your diary.

I *promise* that you are worth it, please make the time.

My notes about this page: ○ Read it   ○ Liked it

....

....

....

....

Hello there, how are you?

I'm going to **expand** a bit on yesterday's post today

It made me think about what we want to achieve and how we are going to achieve those things.

The goals we are going to set ourselves, the plans we will make to achieve those goals, the steps we need to take to complete those plans etc.

As you read the above paragraph, hands up how many of you instantly thought of something related to work or your career? It seems that largely when we talk about achieving goals and making plans, we are talking about our work.

Now, I'm completely on board with the idea that our work needs to fulfill and satisfy us. We do spend the vast majority of our adult life at work, so it's better if we enjoy what we do. But I would like to encourage you all to start thinking about what you want to achieve for your life. Let's start having conversations about the life goals you are going to set yourself, the plans you can make to achieve those goals and the steps you need to take to complete those plans.

Start spreading that conversation out to the people around you.

Today I would like to invite you all to identify one life goal for yourself, that is not related to your work at all, write it on a piece of paper and start thinking about the plan and steps to achieve it.

Enjoy!

My notes about this page: ○ Read it   ○ Liked it

....

....

....

....

Hello all!

As I've told you earlier, my family went on holiday to **France** recently

---

We drove to the Channel tunnel, sat on the train under the sea and then drove ourselves through France.

After an hour or so of driving in France, we realised that things would be simpler if we switched the digital display on the dashboard from miles to kilometres. All the signs were in kilometres and we had no idea how fast we were allowed to go or how far away anything was.

I liked driving in kilometres; they go past faster than miles, you achieve more of them, and you feel as though the journey is easier. They felt lighter than miles. I liked them so much that when we returned to England I left my car display in kilometres for a couple of days.

The thing is, the journeys we made were exactly the same distance, and the roads were exactly the same.

The only difference was how those journeys were measured, in miles or in kilometres. And, how the measurement affected my attitude to the journey. One felt heavy, long and laboured. The other felt swift, light and easy.

I believe that life is the same. It all comes down to how we measure it. Do things feel heavy, long and laboured or swift, light and easy?

How are you measuring situations in your life? In miles or kilometres? And what can you do today to *switch* that attitude around?

My notes about this page: O Read it   O Liked it

....

....

....

....

Hey clubbers.

Think of something you do **every day**

A normal, routine kind of a thing.

Something that you are so used to doing that you don't even have to think about doing it.

Got one? Ace.

Now, do it differently. Find a way to put a twist on it; it doesn't have to be a massive twist, just do it in a different way. For example, every morning I open the curtains in our bedroom before I do girlie things like moisturise and dry my hair. I do it that way round mostly so I can see what I'm doing. This morning I put the light on instead, got myself ready and then opened the curtains.

It's a small thing, but actually I'm telling my subconscious mind that it's not always necessary to keep things the same. I'm demonstrating that change, however small, is possible. The interesting thing for me this morning, is that I was actually ready a bit earlier than normal which gave me time to sort out a bag of clothes for the girls that's been sitting in my bedroom waiting to be sorted for about two weeks now.

So now I've told myself that change is good because I got more done.

Ace, huh?

Do something different today and see what happens.

Enjoy!

My notes about this page: ○ Read it   ○ Liked it

....

....

....

....

Hello everyone, how are you?

Today's post is all about **colour**

I use colours a lot in my work, asking people to visualise different ones for various reasons.

Different colours have different meanings associated with them – red is anger or passion, blue is calming, yellow is happiness, green is balance or growth, purple is the colour of healing and so on.

Now, close your eyes and ask yourself what colour you are today. See what pops into your head. You might see the colour. You might simply get a sense of it. Is this the right colour for you to be today, does it feel good?

If not, what colour does feel good?

Do you need to feel calm or happy or balanced? Take a moment and change that colour around, have a play until you find the one that feels best.

Once you've got the right colour for you, carry it around in your head today. Check in occasionally to see if it has changed at any point or needs adjusting at all. Allow yourself to feel the effects of having that positive colour.

Enjoy!

My notes about this page: O Read it   O Liked it

....

....

....

....

Hi folks!

Over-thinking, huh? **Tiring** isn't it?

My lovely husband has challenged me this morning not to overthink this post, to keep it short and simple.

So, I'm extending that challenge to you today. Catch yourself today, next time you start to over-think and complicate something: stop. Keep it simple today. Give your brain a well deserved rest.

Enjoy!

My notes about this page:　　　　　○ Read it　　○ Liked it

Hi there! How the devil are you?

Have you ever **really** needed the loo?

I mean, *really* needed the loo and been in a place where you have no choice but to wait?

I want you to take a moment and think of how that feels. You get a bit squirmy to start with maybe? Try and distract yourself by talking or singing or doing something? Then you start to feel tense as you hold it together, so to speak. It feels like every muscle in your body is tensing up and you're holding yourself a bit funny, maybe it's affecting the way you are walking? And then you finally make it to the loo and ahhh the relief of letting go... lovely.

Now, imagine feeling that need, that tension, and not allowing yourself to go to the loo. Would it be possible to pretend that it wasn't there? Would it be possible to carry on regardless ad infinitum? Would it be possible to control yourself to that degree?

No, of course it wouldn't, what an absurd suggestion. You would quite literally explode at some point.

And yet folks, we do exactly that, every day, with our emotions. We know they are there, sometimes they make us feel a bit squirmy, and we try and distract ourselves by talking or singing or doing something. We feel tense as we hold it together, our muscles tense up and it starts to affect the way we do things. But we refuse to give ourselves that lovely relief of letting go....

The thing is, the same thing can happen. If we pretend it's not there, carry on regardless and control ourselves to the nth degree, we will at some point explode.

Do yourselves a favour today folks, let go of that tension, let go of that control just a smidge and allow yourself to feel that relief.

Enjoy!

My notes about this page: ○ Read it   ○ Liked it

Hello one and all!

Today we're going back to **gratitude** and **appreciation**

It's a good thing to come back to regularly,
and a fitting way to end this part of the book.

Finding things to be grateful for has a massively positive impact on your brain and the hormones it produces for you.

So, we're doing gratitude again this morning but in a slightly different way. I would like you to think of something you want for yourself for the future. It can be big or small, anything at all.

Close your eyes and get a lovely clear picture of you having that thing. Now, as you picture it, say thank you as if you already have it.

Say thank you as many times as you possibly can, allow yourself to feel the appreciation of and gratitude for that thing as if it is already yours.

I'll tell you a secret. Your subconscious mind has no concept of time. It doesn't know if what you are picturing is past, present or future. So if you act, and feel as if that thing is present, it will join in and make it a reality for you.

Magic, huh?

My notes about this page: ○ Read it   ○ Liked it

Laura's Story

Before I met Jo, I was living a lie...

To everyone else I was bubbly Laura but inside I was an angry, anxious woman in a dark place. I just thought the panic attacks and feelings of highs and lows would go and no way was I going to tell anyone! I was Laura, the loud, confident, bubbly girl!

It was only when I was talking to a close friend about food issues that she pointed out there must be more than just feeling like eating lettuce. Something deeper rooted.

That's when I was introduced to Jo. She worked with me and my problems. Through our sessions, I discovered the real reason I was finding life a struggle and worked on making my mind better.

Then The Happiness Club started. I couldn't wait to sign up. A daily dose of positivity and a better mind-set! Yes, please!

On days that started slow and dull The Happiness Club gave me a huge boost, a new way to picture life or a situation to consider. It really helped me to see things more clearly and less fuzzy.

Anxiety and whirlwinds can be really tiring and I feel so much more alive and energetic because I am training my mind to calm down, take breaths, think clearly and more importantly, to take control and have a choice.

Happiness is a choice and I have learnt through the club's techniques that every day I have a choice. A choice to make my life better, to make it what I want it to be.

Each morning, the post from Jo allows my mind to remember the good in life and what is good in me and around me.

It reminds me to have gratitude for the world around me and remember that I am worth it.

Being in the club has allowed me to face issues in my life to make it better. Everyone is so friendly and adding a comment or a question is never frowned on as everyone has one common goal – happiness.

Looking back on the angry person I was, I can't believe the difference. I still have a way to go, but to get out of that dark place and rebuild me is amazing.

Anxiety and depression are still very taboo subjects but I am so grateful to Jo and The Happiness Club for allowing me to see that life doesn't have to be like that.

Having someone to talk to and support you without judging is important to allow that process to begin and flourish. That is exactly what Jo and the club do by giving you tips each day to help you keep practicing your mind-set.

The Happiness Club is such a unique group. It allows you to face your issues and build your positive mind-set techniques at the same time. I am so grateful to have it in my life.

I'm starting to become the bubbly, happy Laura that everyone thought I was.

Only now I'm not putting on a brave face, I'm actually being me.

Resources

Below are some suggestions of books and websites, that have inspired me along the way, which you may like to peruse further for yourself:

Books:

Ask & It Is Given	*by Esther and Jerry Hicks*
The Power of Now	*by Eckhart Tolle*
You Can Heal Your Life	*by Louise Hay*
The 10-Step Stress Solution	*by Neil Shah*
The Biology of Belief	*by Bruce Lipton*
You Are The Placebo	*by Dr Joe Dispenza*
The Four Agreements	*by Don Miguel Ruiz*
The Mindfulness Breakthrough	*by Sarah Silverton*
Mindfulness	*by Mark Williams and Danny Penman*
How To Succeed in Life & Happiness	*by Jeff Spires*
Your Flight To Happiness	*by Toni Mackenzie*
In Praise of Slow	*by Carl Honoré*

Websites:

www.abraham-hicks.com

www.actionforhappiness.org

www.wiseattention.org

www.mindfulnessinaction.co.uk

www.carlhonore.com

And, of course: www.thehappinessclub.co.uk

Acknowledgments

To all those people I couldn't have produced this book without:

Jen Hinds: www.jenhinds.com

For her invaluable advice and support with the creation
and branding of The Happiness Club.

Jo Swift: www.JoSwiftProofreadingServices.co.uk

For her wonderful work proofreading the contents of this book.

Alex Platt: www.swiftva.co.uk

For her help, support, guidance and general brilliant-ness.

Kirstie Edwards: www.kirstieedwards.co.uk

The world's best photographer.

Trevor Howarth

For his beautiful design, branding and layout work.

Sue Miller: www.allwordsmatter.co.uk

For editing and rather brilliantly guiding me through the minefield
of publishing and promoting my first book.

About the Author

Jo Howarth is a Mindfulness Practitioner & Advanced Hypnotherapist living in Merseyside. She suffered from stress and anxiety for many years and now teaches the tools that brought her through to the sunny side of life.

Jo runs the monthly membership club that is The Happiness Club as well as helping people on an individual basis through private sessions. She offers businesses the chance to have their own Corporate Happiness Programme and she visits schools to run the School Happiness Programme for children of all ages and the staff that teach them. She works and speaks all over the UK.

Jo is happily married to Trev and they have two beautiful daughters. She enjoys nothing more than spending time with her family and encourages as many people as possible to do the same.

You can find out more about Jo's work here:

www.thehappinessclub.co.uk

You can also sign up for **a free one month trial** of The Happiness Club here:

www.thehappinessclub.co.uk/free-trial/

LinkedIn: Jo Howarth

Twitter: @HappinessClubJo

Facebook: www.facebook.com/TheHappinessClubLtd/

Printed in Great Britain
by Amazon